PIAGET
FOR BEGINNERS®

ADRIANA SERULNIKOV

ILLUSTRATED BY RODRIGO SUÁREZ

Writers and Readers®

Writers and Readers Publishing, Inc.
P.O. Box 461, Village Station, New York, NY 10014
sales@forbeginners.com

Writers and Readers Ltd.
PO Box 29522, London N1 8FB England
begin@writersandreaders.com

Spanish Edition:
Jean Piaget para principiantes
published by ERA NASCIENTE SLR
Arce 287, Buenos Aires (1426) Argentina

Publishing FOR BEGINNERS® books continuously since 1975

1975: Cuba • 1976: Marx • 1977: Lenin • 1978: Nuclear Power • 1979: Einstein • Freud • 1980: Mao Trotsky • 1981: Capitalism • 1982: Darwin • Economists • French Revolution • Marx's Kapital Food • Ecology • 1983: DNA • Ireland • 1984: London • Peace • Medicine • Orwell • Reagan • Nicaragua Black History • 1985: Marx's Diary • 1986: Zen • Psychiatry • Reich • Socialism • Computers Brecht • Elvis • 1988: Architecture • Sex • JFK • Virginia Woolf • 1990: Nietzsche • Plato Malcolm X • Judaism • 1991: WW II • Erotica • African History • 1992: Philosophy • Rainforests Miles Davis • Islam • Pan Africanism • 1993: Psychiatry • Black Women • Arabs & Israel • Freud 1994: Babies • Foucault • Heidegger • Hemingway • Classical Music • 1995: Jazz • Jewish Holocaust Health Care • Domestic Violence • Sartre • United Nations • Black Holocaust • Black Panthers Martial Arts • History of Clowns • 1996: Opera • Biology • Saussure • UNICEF • Kierkegaard Addiction & Recovery • I Ching • Buddha • Derrida • Chomsky • McLuhan • Jung • 1997: Lacan Shakespeare • Structuralism • Che • 1998: Fanon • Adler • Gandhi • U.S. Constitution • 1999: The Body • Krishnamurti • English Language • Postmodernism • Scotland • Wales • Castaneda • Gestalt

CONTENTS

'I must admit I'm dying of curiosity...'

Some things have changed in schools. For example, many teachers use children's mistakes to indicate how they may be helped to improve rather than treating them simply as errors to be punished. We also try to understand their ideas before they start learning, so that we can create useful situations in class. Where does all this come from? From Piaget's genetic psychology.

When our eldest child was a baby, I remember spending a lot of time wondering what stage of development he had reached. But with the youngest everything was much easier. We made sure that he had enough stimulation is his life—things to smell, to shake, to bite—well, to explore the world! And yes, I suppose that, in a way, Piaget's influence has also affected families.

It's 1976. Jean Piaget, the greatest representative of the psychologists of the Geneva school and the creator of **genetic psychology**, reaches 80 years of age. He is surrounded by the affection and gratitude of his collaborators and disciples, who have travelled from various parts of the world for this occasion. For almost 70 years, Piaget has researched and published endless works, all characterised by a rare coherence and fluency. At 80 he continues to work tirelessly, and big projects are still being planned.

Four years later, on 16 September 1980, he died in Geneva, the city where he had spent most of his hard-working life.

It all began in Neuchâtel, a French–speaking Swiss canton...

Jean had been interested in animal life from an early age. He was soon a young expert on those fossils and molluscs to be found in the Swiss lakes. This anticipated the passion for scientific investigation which he would bring to his whole life. He spent most of his young life studying molluscs under the fascinated direction of **Dr Paul Godet**, Director of the Neuchâtel Museum of Natural History, and he very soon became his assistant. When he was 11 years old Jean published his first article in a specialist magazine. This, like all his writing until he was 18, was based on meticulous observations, especially of the processes of adaptation in animal life.

2 Piaget by Piaget

I was born in 1896 in the bosom of a well-off and cultured family.

My father was a man with a meticulous and critical nature. A historian, he gave lectures on medieval literature at the University. From him I learned the value of detailed, systematic work.

My mother was intelligent and energetic, but had a difficult temperament which made our family life complicated. I believe that because of this, I imitated my father and took refuge in intellectual work very early on.

I worked twice a week for the naturalist Godet from the time I was 11 until his death 4 years later. Every Saturday afternoon, half an hour before my teacher came, I used to be there waiting for him!

After Godet's death, I published a series of works which produced some amusing responses.

We would be very pleased to include you as one of our collaborators.

Director of the Geneva Natural History Museum

Dear colleague,
We would be very interested to meet you for an exchange of ideas.

If only they knew how old I am! They would ignore me...like that editor who, when he found out my age a few days ago, no longer wanted to publish my articles.

As premature and imperfect as these studies were, they were very useful for my scientific development. I had the rare privilege of discovering science before going through the trauma of adolescence.

Vocational crisis: Jean will become a naturalist, however...

Family crisis: his Protestant mother is pushing for Jean to receive 'religious instruction'. His father does not believe in religion, being attached to the ideas of historical truth.

Religious crisis: proof of the existence of God is very weak.

Emotional crisis: he is disturbed by the horrors of World War I.

Intellectual crisis: religious dogma cannot be reconciled with either biology or rational thought.

I remember with affection the holidays spent on Lake Annency with my godfather, a French-speaking man of letters. By engaging me in enlightening conversation, he tried to channel my interest in biology towards philosophy very early on. Listening for the first time to someone who was not a theologist talk about philosophy made a great impression on me.

Yes, the problem of knowledge is the key! But Bergson disappoints me. He isn't proving his theories empirically, he is only speculating.

It was on one of those summer afternoons that I had an intense revelation the clarity of which made me almost ecstatic: God equals Life and the explanation of all things (including the spiritual) lies in biology. A little later, a conviction came to me which led me towards my ultimate goal.

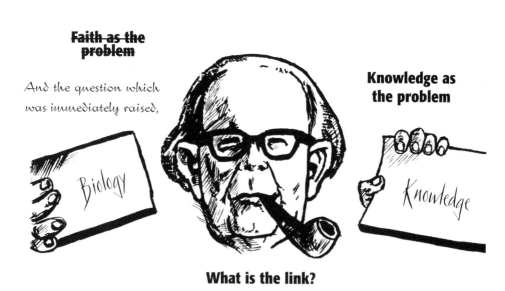

Faith as the problem

And the question which was immediately raised,

Knowledge as the problem

What is the link?

...gave the following answer: PSYCHOLOGY
That was when my adolescent dreams led me towards a fixed horizon:
I would dedicate my life to the bio-logic of knowledge.

While I was finishing my baccalaureate I read and wrote feverishly. During this time I discovered that to be able to think and organise my ideas, it was essential for me to write, and this remained valid for the rest of my professional life. In endless notebooks I constructed what I call my 'philosophical system'.

In the absence of basic experimental opportunities, I tried to give expression to what remained a theoretical system in a philosophical novel, 'Recherche'. I had been forced to take a year off and to spend it resting in the mountains in order to regain my health after exhausting myself. This gave me the opportunity to write.

'Recherche' means:
'search–investigation'

This novel contains the basic ideas which will form the theoretical nucleus of his future work.

13

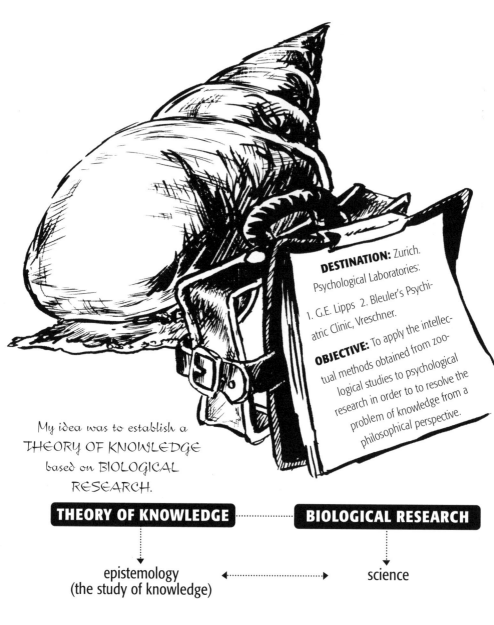

DESTINATION: Zurich. Psychological Laboratories: 1. G.E. Lipps 2. Bleuler's Psychiatric Clinic, Vreschner.

OBJECTIVE: To apply the intellectual methods obtained from zoological studies to psychological research in order to to resolve the problem of knowledge from a philosophical perspective.

My idea was to establish a THEORY OF KNOWLEDGE based on BIOLOGICAL RESEARCH.

THEORY OF KNOWLEDGE	**BIOLOGICAL RESEARCH**
epistemology (the study of knowledge)	science

In Zurich I read Freud and attended lectures by Pfister and Jung. However, at this time I didn't manage to discover a basis for research with which to resolve the problems I had set myself. A little disillusioned, I decided to return to Switzerland, where I spent some time. In the autumn of 1919, I began another journey, this time to Paris.

But the most important thing that happened to me in Paris was that Théophile Simon encouraged me to accept a job in Alfred Binet's laboratory. I had to conduct intelligence tests that had been devised by the two scientists with Parisian children.

I made use of the autonomy I had been given and began to hold personal, clinical interviews with the children to investigate in depth the reasoning which led them to commit what adults would initially call 'errors'.

My area of investigation was finally defined. This marked the end of a theoretical period and the beginning of my dedication to experimental psychology, through which I could get answers to my epistemological questions.

I was therefore able to establish that logical reasoning is not innate. Knowledge continues to develop as a process in which the child interacts with his environment. How do we acquire the capacity for understanding? We do this in the interaction which is established between:

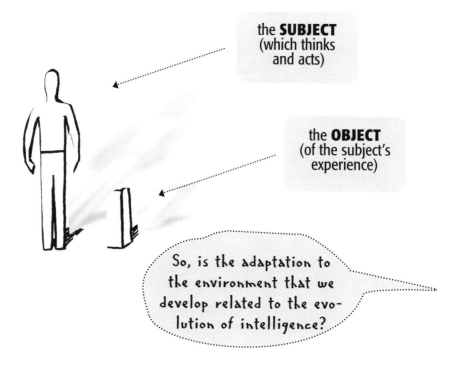

the **SUBJECT**
(which thinks
and acts)

the **OBJECT**
(of the subject's
experience)

So, is the adaptation to the environment that we develop related to the evolution of intelligence?

I made it clear that I intended to construct a theory on this point.

Theory of knowledge
epistemology

based on ·····································▶ **Biological investigation**
science

I could now develop this into:

Theory of knowledge
epistemology

based on ·····································▶ **The study of its origin (evolution)**
genetics

Was Piaget the first to be so preoccupied with studying knowledge?

Although Jean Piaget was not the first or the last epistemologist, the way in which he approached the problem was absolutely original. Let's see why...

It is very difficult to know when humanity began to ask itself...

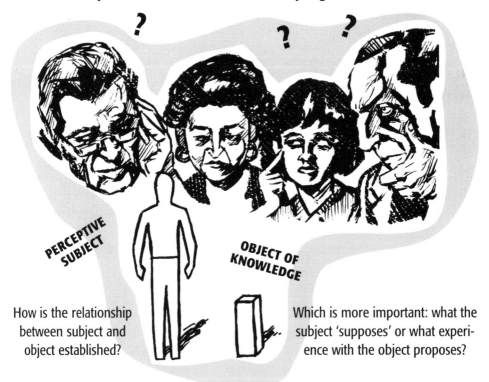

PERCEPTIVE SUBJECT

OBJECT OF KNOWLEDGE

How is the relationship between subject and object established?

Which is more important: what the subject 'supposes' or what experience with the object proposes?

If one traces the influences on Western thought back to their origins, one arrives at the classic philosophers and the preoccupations which exercised their minds. It was with them that the two great philosophical currents were born which so affected the understanding of knowledge.

RATIONALISM (= the predominance of reason)
EMPIRICISM (= the predominance of experience)

The rationalists' argument

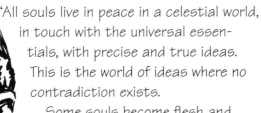

'All souls live in peace in a celestial world, in touch with the universal essentials, with precise and true ideas. This is the world of ideas where no contradiction exists.

Some souls become flesh and arrive in the earthly world formed by material objects. But before they get there, they go through Lethe, the River of Oblivion, which is why they arrive here in a state of amnesia, of apparent ignorance.

Knowledge constitutes itself by a slow process. The soul will then awaken to knowledge that has remained dormant: knowledge acquired earlier, during that passage through the world of ideas.'

Plato (428-347)

How can we interpret Plato's myth?

IDEA 1 The individual is born with knowledge (it is innate).

IDEA 2 The individual needs a stimulus to 'be awakened' (reality).

IDEA 3 The individual is the basic medium of knowledge.

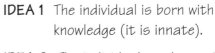

Other rationalists followed **Plato: Descartes, Spinosa, Leibniz...**

The empiricists' argument

**ARISTOTLE
(384–322 BC)**

When man is born he is a 'tabula rasa' (a clean slate) upon which will be etched significant impressions, the product of his interaction with objects.

IDEA 1 The subject is born ignorant.

IDEA 2 The subject gains knowledge only through experiencing his five senses, therefore, there is no knowledge without experience.

IDEA 3 The object is the basic medium of knowledge.

Aristotle was followed by other empiricists: **Saint Thomas, Locke, Berkeley, Hume...**

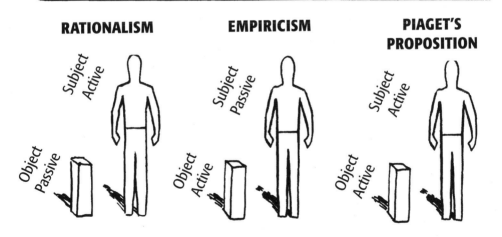

In Piaget's interaction both the subject and the object construct each other. How? By action and through a process.

The grand hypothesis that Jean Piaget sets out is that the spontaneous way in which children build their knowledge is parallel to the evolution of scientific knowledge.

From Freud to Piaget: theoretical controversy

FREUD

Psychoanalysis, as a theory of the psychic mechanism, included diverse theoretical elements: dreams, fantasies, representation, failures etc...

I started from very insignificant phenomena, things that were unrelated to the science of my time; failures for example.

I destroyed the illusion of infantile innocence. Sexuality, from the psychic point of view, begins at birth.

PIAGET

Genetic psychology, as a theory of knowledge, makes it possible to understand concepts such as: perception, learning, spatial organisation etc...

In my day children's mistakes were rejected by experimental psychology; only the correct answers were considered.

Children acquire knowledge in a similar way to scientists. Children's knowledge is not innocent. They are not a tabula rasa.

Children: 'little scientists'

Piaget believed that the way in which scientists build their theories is similar to the way in which children learn about the world. Therefore, if he were able to reconstruct this process experimentally, he would be able to formulate epistemological hypotheses that would be, of course, scientific.

What nonsense, asking children questions which give scientists sleepless nights!

By the way, isn't the little that children know taught to them by adults?

Why do things fall down?

Why do some children starve?

What is a number?

Why do some things sink in water and others float?

What is death?

Why do children have to go to school?

Children are always asking questions and creating hypotheses in an attempt to explain reality. They look for 'constants' or rules which help them to understand the way things function, the events that are part of their lives.

24

In summer there are peaches and mum buys them from the greengrocer. In winter, I can eat tinned peaches...

At last! He understands!

Not only do they replace one hypothesis with a better one, but sometimes they even produce integrated syntheses, just like scientists.

SCIENTIST

Children produce hypotheses, try to back them up, manage to change them under certain conditions, and follow a direction in their research...

Oh!... What a coincidence!

Children, like scientists, try to explain reality in relation to their reference points. The difference is that for each child the reference points are going to be different. There are, besides, other differences and similarities...

SCIENTISTS

- ✔ their profession is knowledge;
- ✔ hold hypotheses (which are supposed to work) that are conscious and explicit;
- ✔ are familiar with physics, maths and history;
- ✔ know the history of their discipline;
- ✔ use the appropriate methodology;
- ✔ are able to start from theoretical abstractions and complex experiments;
- ✔ work within an ideological, conceptual and technological framework

CHILDREN

- ✔ know things, but not because of a profession;
- ✔ try to explain the world;
- ✔ play, explore, try things out, choose, correct, reject, discover;
- ✔ hold hypotheses which are not conscious and they need help to explain them;
- ✔ begin from their experiences and the knowledge they already have;
- ✔ work within an everyday context.

So, what interested Jean Piaget in children was...

✔ what makes one child different from another.

✔ their emotional development.

✔ their psycho-sexual development.

✔ what one expects from them in relation to their age.

✔ their social development.

✔ the substance of their ideas.

✔ **how they go about constructing their knowledge of the world.**

Is knowledge 'constructed'?

Yes. The concept of the stability of matter is one of the first problems that physicists tackled. Isn't that right? Alright, an epistemologist who asks himself about the origin of this concept could affirm that this comes from experience or else from reasoning...

Sure! It depends on who replies.

O.K. If we trace the cognitive history of children, we can identify the moment at which they manage to establish that matter is conserved, even under varying conditions.

How did he manage to work out the concept of the permanence of substance?

If you explore the route by which children arrive at this notion you will come across some interesting epistemological answers.

Does this mean that: Aristotle thought like a child, Galileo like a primary school child and Newton like a university student?

No. We have already seen that such an analogy doesn't exist in the context of thought, but in the functioning, the mechanism, the process through which knowledge is generated. Besides, the history of science has no end. In the same way, cognitive development begins at birth and continues with the acquisition of formal thought.

4 Genetic psychology

So how was genetic psychology born?

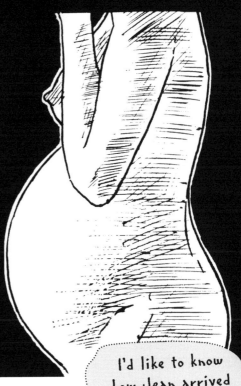

THE PREDICTABLE

- from psychological questions
- from clinical concerns
- from educational questions

THE UNPREDICTABLE

- from epistemological questions

I'd like to know how Jean arrived at this point...

Genetic psychology attained, through the research promoted by Jean Piaget and his colleagues, a level of development equivalent to other branches of psychology, such as child psychology, and including general psychology. However, the discoveries they made during their experimental research into the acquisition of knowledge by children, help to resolve epistemological-philosophical problems.

Piaget searched obsessively to explain psychologically the mechanism by which causal relationships are established between facts and the carrying out of logical tasks.

THE RESULT

VALENTINE

They launched an extensive programme of theoretical development with the help of students from the Institute. Among them was Valentine Châtenay, who was soon to become his wife and faithful collaborator. They married in 1923.

J. PIAGET
THE LANGUAGE AND THOUGHT OF THE CHILD

JEAN PIAGET
JUDGMENT AND REASONING IN THE CHILD

THE CHILD'S CONCEPTION OF THE WORLD
Jean Piaget

THE MORAL JUDGMENT OF THE CHILD
J. PIAGET

THE CHILD'S CONCEPTION OF PHYSICAL CAUSALITY
Jean Piaget

In six years Piaget published five preliminary books, with the intention that the concepts expressed in them would later be shaped into

I haven't organised my ideas yet and although many people already agree with them, others criticise them. However, it would be absurd to tell the most critical 'wait a bit, you haven't seen what is yet to come', especially since even I don't know...

THE CONSEQUENCES

BELGIUM   USA   SPAIN   SWITZER   FRANCE   HOLLAND   GREE

It was naive to think that these first publications wouldn't be taken into account. In addition, I was too young to know that for a long while one is judged by one's first works and only the very assiduous reader will consult the most recent.

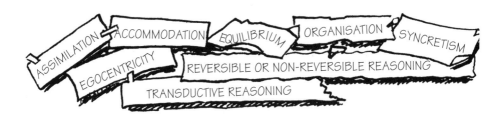

ASSIMILATION   ACCOMMODATION   EQUILIBRIUM   ORGANISATION   SYNCRETISM
EGOCENTRICITY   REVERSIBLE OR NON-REVERSIBLE REASONING
TRANSDUCTIVE REASONING

In spite of the reservations that Piaget himself had about these works, the fundamental concepts of his theory took shape in them and they acquired a certain unexpected popularity.

What are these concepts?

Don't worry, it will all be explained to you later.

Although Piaget believed that thought proceeds from action, in the first stage of the research they had concentrated on conversations with the children, and the language through which we could understand a child's logic.

LUCIENNE

JACQUELINE

LAURENT

You see? If I had started my research by studying the first years of life, I would have avoided most of the criticisms of my first works.

With the birth of his children and in their first two years of life, Piaget began a phase of intense observation which allowed him to confirm, in a practical way, that which he had previously discovered through language.

My first serious books began with the observation of my own children. Jacqueline, Lucienne and Laurent were the main characters. Studying the birth of intelligence and the construction of reality, I came across my initial ideas again: the continuity between the organic and the rational.

Do these three books have a special value because of this?

Of course they do! They are the basic trilogy if you want to understand anything about genetic psychology.

Origins of Intelligence in Children, 1936

The Child's Construction of Reality, 1937

Mental Imagery in the Child, 1946

Are they easy to read?

No. The explanations are complicated. However, the description of numerous observations makes it easier to study.

Intelligence comes before language

 What do you know?
How do you know?

 How do you move from
one stage to another?

The origins of logic cannot be attributed to language. The first two years of life are marked by an intense mental development. More than that: there is a real logic existing before the appearance of language, substantiated by the actions that the subject makes.

Just the opposite of what the rationalists think! I feel vindicated because I see that Piaget has returned to his first love. He continues to state that there is a continuity between physiological organisation (life forms) and psychological organisation (structures of thought).

Piaget soon found it useful to change the clinical method that he had used in his research until then. Instead of mere verbalisations, he would direct the questions towards objects that the children could manipulate.

A time of collaboration and production

Teams of assistants and colleagues didn't merely collect data, but took an increasingly active part in the way the experimental programme was carried out.

One learns through teaching. Parallel to the research, I developed an intense teaching programme during those years: Psychology of the Child, Philosophy of Science, History of Scientific Thought, Sociology... My epistemological and interdisciplinary vocation was clear.

After 30 years of research we have shown that the ability to understand a reversible action, a property which characterises the operation of logical intelligence, that is to say, mature intelligence, is not acquired all at once, but in the course of a series of successive stages.

I hope one day to be able to demonstrate that relationships exist between the development of mental structures and stages of emotional development. It would culminate in a general theory of structures, to which my previous studies would constitute only an introduction.

I am saying this at 50 years of age and realise that 16 years ago I was still very young... In fact, I'd like to explain exactly what I've become...

Today it's still too early to achieve the goal that I set myself in those days. Meanwhile I must go on with the research. However, I can support the proposition that a convergence exists between the problems and the solutions found in biology and those being considered in the field of intelligence. For example, adaptation, development, etc.

There are those who think that the period of 1935-1955 was the most fruitful and original of Piaget's work.

It's quite probable, but in any case this was only possible thanks to COLLABORATION. I'll tell you why...

Switzerland had remained neutral during World War II. Anyway, being over 40 years old, I was exempt from any military service. As an intellectual, I couldn't do anything else except carry on working...

France was under Nazi occupation, when the scientist, **Henri Piéron**, invited Piaget to teach a course at the Collège de France.

I feel honoured to have been invited to work with you all, my friends and colleagues who are united in opposition.

The course gave rise to the book which his students affectionately called 'the little intelligence', because Piaget's editor decided to publish it in a pocket edition. *The Psychology of Intelligence* (1947) formed the first synthesis of their work and was published in innumerable languages.

The sudden death of Edouard Claparède, made Piaget his successor at the Laboratory of Experimental Psychology in the J.J.Rousseau Institute. The fact that it had wonderful research facilities available soon bore fruit.

We harvested the product of a long period of gestation of our ideas and in addition we took the right decision to study older children, with the aim of tracing the complete origin of the fundamental categories of thought.

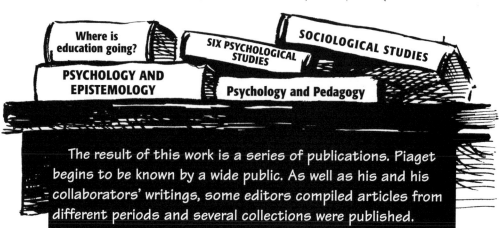

Where is education going?

SIX PSYCHOLOGICAL STUDIES

SOCIOLOGICAL STUDIES

PSYCHOLOGY AND EPISTEMOLOGY

Psychology and Pedagogy

The result of this work is a series of publications. Piaget begins to be known by a wide public. As well as his and his collaborators' writings, some editors compiled articles from different periods and several collections were published.

The cause of Genetic Psychology acquired worthy collaborators. **Bärbel Inhelder** stood out as the best of these. and it is difficult to imagine Piaget's epistemology without the existence of Inhelder.

Bärbel Inhelder had been his fellow researcher in psychological studies. Together they started to study again the problems of the psychological mechanisms which underlie logical and causal reasoning.

The responsibility for the psychological research that Inhelder took on allowed Piaget to concentrate once again on epistemological questions.

Together we supervise and make sense of all the research of various scientists who were working in associated research centres. All these investigations are strongly linked, both in theory and in methodology.

They conducted three types of investigation:

1. into the development of perception in order to understand its relation with intelligence and to put the Gestalt theory to the test. Publication: *The Mechanisms of Perception*, 1961;

2. into the origin of the ideas. Publications: *The Child's Conception of Number, The Origin of the idea of Chance in Children, The Development of the Concept of Space in the Child*, etc;

3. into logical mathematical structures, which characterise mental operations and which have already been converted into a tool to analyse the distinct behaviour of children at similar levels of development. Piaget was helped by the work of **Alina Szeminska** and **Seymour Papert**, with their studies of cybernetics and artificial intelligence.

Jean Piaget

THE MECHANISMS OF PERCEPTION

ORIGINS OF INTELLIGENCE IN CHILDREN

THE CHILD'S CONCEPTION OF NUMBER

The key work synthesizing Piaget's thought in this period is:

1947

THE PSYCHOLOGY OF INTELLIGENCE

The war over, Piaget dedicated time to the task of supporting a number of international organisations. He represented UNESCO, for example, at a conference held in Rio de Janeiro.

I can state that we worked together feverishly, with the elation of the post-war period, and at the same time with the fear that the international situation would deteriorate again.

Piaget had planned to dedicate five years to the psychology of the child and ended up giving thirty. He was fascinated by this work, but the time came to bring it to a conclusion. This was done in a general work which analyses the mechanism of the acquisition of knowledge, not by statistical means, but from the point of view of growth and development.

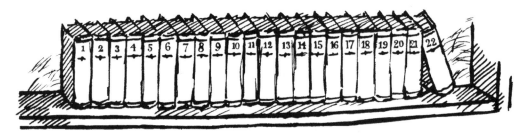

His ideas, expressed in various ways in twenty-two volumes, was this: the intellectual operations conform to and function like linking structures and these structures, which have their roots in biological morphogenesis itself, express themselves in distinct types of equilibrium.

Evolution therefore is a total system which is at once organic, psychological and social, and tends to attain a kind of equilibrium. This means that when we manage to find a structure that is useful, it tends to remain stable, at least for a while.

One of Piaget's outstanding works was his **Introduction to Genetic Epistemology**. In 1950 he published these three volumes which represent an extensive presentation of his programme of work.

1950 The framework of Genetic Psychology has already been built. From now on, until 1980 (when Piaget died) his theory will be enriched, elaborated and completed, but without being substantially altered.

To think in order to write, to write in order to think

FINISHED PAGE = PUBLISHABLE PAGE

I try to write by putting myself in the position of a reader who knows nothing about our research. I must be clear and precise.

TO WRITE A BOOK... YOU JUST HAVE TO START, AND THE REST WILL FOLLOW AUTOMATICALLY.

Every night I leave a phrase unfinished, to be picked up again next morning.

BUT IT IS SO DIFFICULT TO WRITE LETTERS!

I'm always behind with my correspondence. I find it very difficult to reply to letters, especially when the content is purely bureaucratic.

Small rucksack for collecting interesting plant specimens

I am an insatiable walker. One of my favourite walks is climbing up the Salève, a French mountain on the edge of the city of Geneva.

Peasant hands (not a writer's) which grow rare species

During the holidays I take refuge in the mountains, in the forest regions of the Valais in a mountain hut at 1,000 metres, which can't be reached by any means of communication. For several weeks I write on improvised tables after taking pleasant walks.

Heavy walking boots

Going up

▲ notes gathered by the assistants over the year

▲ texts to finish

▲ ideas to develop

Coming down

▼ manuscripts ready for publication

▼ Experimental research projects for the next months

His days were organised in a regulated manner. Every day he found time to think, in the calm that contact with nature gave him. Later he would spend hours writing.

In the morning he worked with other people...

I'm very fond of the company of young and intelligent colleagues. Their comments are very stimulating.

In the afternoons he would go for walks and peacefully put his ideas together, organise them and return to his desk at his home in the suburbs.

The office in Jean Piaget's house

But how do you manage to find any of your work, sir?

I look for it. I spend less time doing that than I would tidying up every day.

Where does the desk begin or end?

The only free space is a path between the door and his chair.

The only few centimetres of free space are for putting small hand-written sheets of paper on.

Books and papers pile up from floor to ceiling.

This is the fruit of years of accumulated mess: I call it my 'essential order'.

Dr Jean Piaget, famous Swiss scientist, has been named Director of the 'International Office of Education'.

From then on, his administrative and international tasks multiplied.

> But how did that happen, Jean? I thought you were interested in teaching questions?

> That's true. This body, which later became closely related to UNESCO, made me think about educational problems, although these have always been on the edge of my interests. I recognise that there was a rather adventurous element in this undertaking.

> We must thank the Rockefeller Foundation for its support, without which I, as the representative of the people of Geneva, couldn't have set up our Science Faculty in 1956.

With the funding from the Rockefeller Foundation which approved Piaget's research project, plus that from the Swiss Fund for Scientific Research, the International Centre of Genetic Epistemology was set up in 1955. The Centre pulled together a multi-disciplinary team of scientists to investigate epistemological problems over the academic year.

We are looking for a common task for the researchers and their respective teams, which they will carry out over several years. Bärbel Inhelder or I will hold meetings with the researchers to feed back the results of their work. Generally I am in charge of writing up the results that are then checked by others and inspire new projects. This will continue until we feel we have nothing else to discover.

They studied, for example, the development of numbers using the **clinical-critical** questionnaire* with a sample group of children. At the end of the year, at a symposium to which world specialists in the subject were invited, they discussed the work, and made provisional conclusions and decided which subject to study in the next phase.

Participating in joint research with specialists from very different disciplines, constantly bringing together the theoretical test and the experimental analysis, was an exciting adventure. The annual results were published in a journal, **Studies of Genetic Epistemology**, which runs into numerous volumes. In just one year they published the first four volumes of the journal.

*see 'the clinical method' p73.

6 Academic recognition

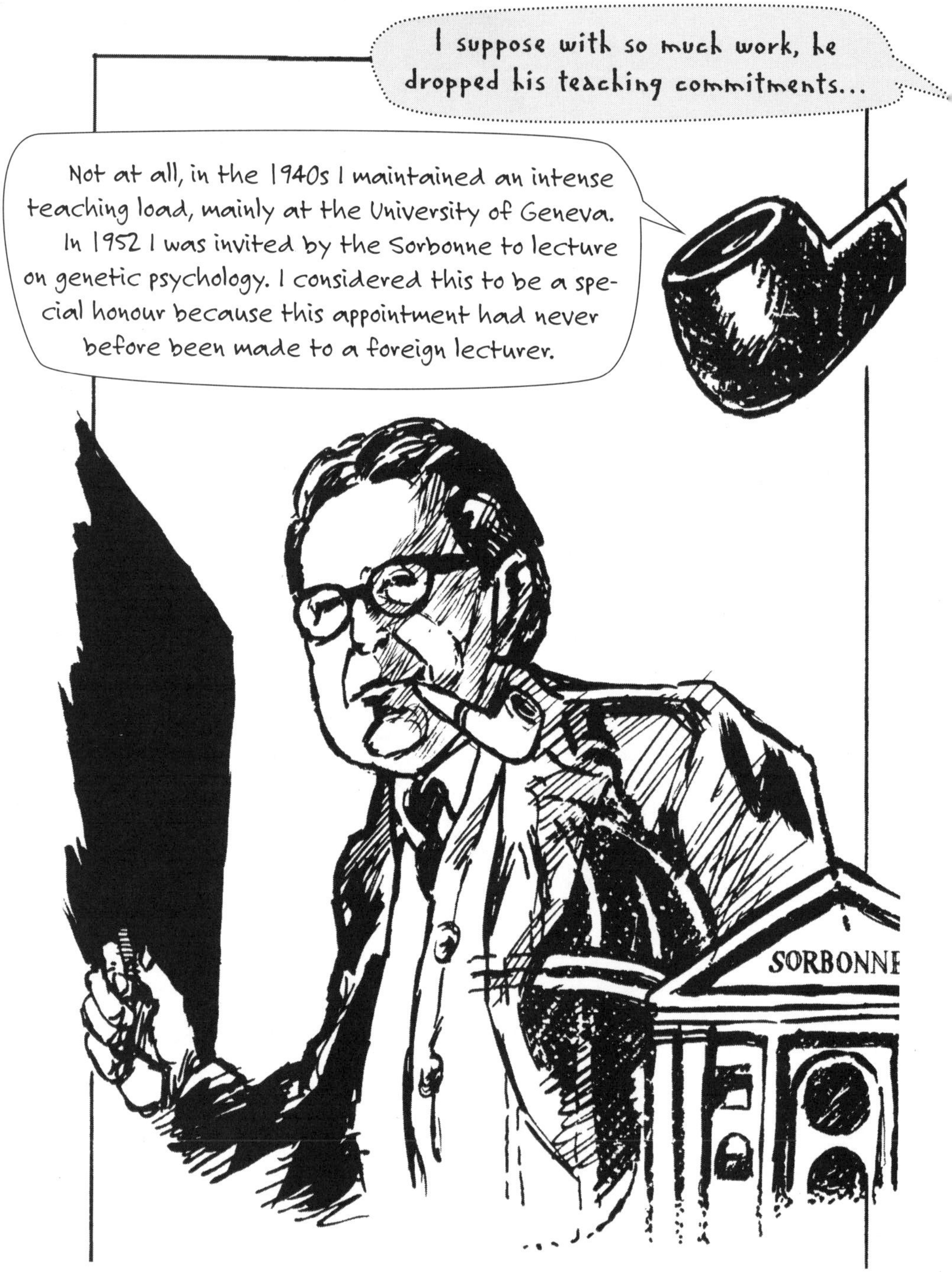

The University had to modify its main lecture hall to accommodate the growing numbers of students who wanted to attend Piaget's lectures.

Clock to keep strict control of the time of the classes without rushing and while still respecting the students' rhythm.

Envelopes with foreign stamps that contain manuscripts on small and yellowing sheets.

An even clearer exponent than his books, he was precise, and able to flesh out explanations without pushing the conclusions of an idea, or body of ideas, too far.

Finally in 1963, due to the intense activity generated in the Centre of Genetic Epistemology he had to give up teaching which he enjoyed so much and which had given him such intellectual enrichment.

He was a doctor *honoris causa* of the Sorbonne and previously he had been honoured with the same title at Harvard, during the tricentennial celebrations of the University. He had also been honoured by the Universities of Brussels, Oslo, Warsaw, Cambridge, Manchester, Brazil and other prestigious centres of study

The most rewarding experience was to have become a member of the New York Academy of Sciences.

Yet he did not abandon his research with molluscs and plants because of his twenty honorary doctorates. He continued to study the relationship between hereditary structures and the environment although giving it somewhat less time.

In 1966 Piaget reaches 70 years of age and there are a great many celebrations in his honour. The 18th International Congress of Psychology, meeting in Moscow, and counting on his presence, pays homage to him.

In 1971 Piaget reaches retirement age. At 75, now relieved of his teaching duties, he puts his energy into the activities of the Centre of Genetic Epistemology. Although there is a tendency among the scientists of the Centre to concentrate on genetic psychology, the goal of the research, under his guidance, is still **epistemological issues**.

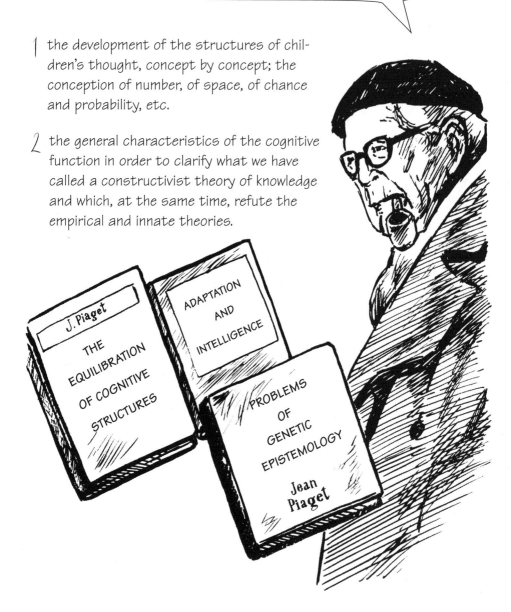

Most of the psychogenetic studies that we have completed are divided into two phases:

1 the development of the structures of children's thought, concept by concept; the conception of number, of space, of chance and probability, etc.

2 the general characteristics of the cognitive function in order to clarify what we have called a constructivist theory of knowledge and which, at the same time, refute the empirical and innate theories.

These books, together with others produced by the Centre, are published in the collection **Genetic Epistemology** and are an accurate record of the subject matter developed over the previous years. In the 1970s, the **Jean Piaget Archives** were created, with the intention of collecting together all his work and that of his collaborators.

7 Constructivism: a matter of learning

In the 1960s, The International Centre of Genetic Epistemology takes on the problem of learning.

> What do their studies show?

If you want a child to learn, you have to know at least two laws:

1 Children have (even without knowing it) a previous logic before going to school;

> Is that bad?

> No, but their potential will condition their learning at school, so this has to be borne in mind.

2 The level of organisation of their thought is regulated by laws that will determine how and when they will learn and the extent of their learning.

> Wasn't it the other way round?

> No, the empiricists are wrong about this.

Learning is a process of building. The subject doesn't limit herself to receiving stimulation and reacting automatically to it. On the contrary, she begins to use what she has learned and starts to interact with the object she has to learn about. She learns actively.

• Which psychological processes allow one to move from one determined structural level to another higher level?

• Is it possible to carry out operational learning, that is to say: to accelerate the acquisition of determined operational notions? To what extent and with what limitations? And what would be the procedures?

In the 1970s, Inhelder, **Sinclair**, **Bovet** and other disciples of Piaget were busy providing answers to these questions, with a fundamental constructivist focus.

If we could speed up cognitive development, under certain experimental conditions, we would have the possibility of identifying the mechanisms that are responsible for intellectual development.

That's what they had been seeking for years.

Yes. The phase we are approaching is that of the functional aspects of the cognitive process, as demonstrated in LEARNING AND STRUCTURES OF KNOWLEDGE, 1974.

The basic ideas of Piaget's work don't owe their genesis to particular theories or authors, but originate in Piaget's own ideas which he sketched out when he was 20.

It is difficult to find any psychologist that influenced Piaget's theory. The only one we could mention is **Pierre Janet**, with his theory on the conception of thought as a consequence of action. This idea was then developed systematically by Piaget.

> Wasn't the Gestalt theory the origin of your explanation of organised structures, from the equilibrium between the whole and its parts?

> The Gestalt theorists and myself worked together on these ideas and when they began to publish I realised that there were some partial coincidences between their proposals and ours.

PIAGET'S THEORY = A BUILDING WITH ITS OWN STRUCTURE

The more one compares Piaget's psychological theories with others, the clearer they become. They form a system of conceptualisation that:

1 allows the integration of the data from other theories, and

2 is resistant to being integrated into the conceptualisation of other theories.

Has anyone attempted to adapt the concepts of psychogenesis to another theory?

Dr Daniel Berlyne, the famous neo-conductivist, tried to reduce the operational concept of intelligence to a stimulus-response concept, as put forward by Clark Hull.

This simplification re-minds me of a conversation between a mother and her son...

No it's not, it's a grey kitten.

It's a big brown dog.

Look: it's got cat's whiskers, it's small and grey.

No! It's a big brown dog.

Yes, but I cut its whiskers, gave it long legs, and made it grow.

Berlyne didn't cut the whiskers or alter the colour, but what he did was to change the theory of learning.

I must, without doubt, be the most criticised psychologist of the century. My view is that when criticism and argument go hand in hand they become a system of mutual control.

I don't pay great attention to my old critics. They have mostly concentrated on what was left out of the theory rather than what it was proposing. Moreover there were other people who took care to refute them.

Some critics become colleagues, or just redo their experiments, adjusting them to Piaget's interpretations.

I'll repeat this time and again: the coherence and the growing credibility of our theory is due to continuous collaboration and not to the solitary work of an individual researcher.

Curiously, the process of working as an interdisciplinary team was also the subject of criticism from orthodox psychologists.

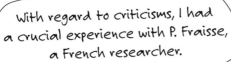

With regard to criticisms, I had a crucial experience with P. Fraisse, a French researcher.

Fraisse had doubts about some of their results, especially in relation to the notions of speed and time, in which fields he was a specialist.

Let's each duplicate the other's experiments and compare the results.

Let's do the critical analysis together before publication and we should be sure of understanding each other.

The disagreements soon gave way to these practices, crucial for both of them. Moreover, a solid friendship was born between them.

I regret not having had sustained contact with certain scholars. How good, for example, it would be to share with the logician E.W.Beth!

On the other hand, he didn't find certain criticisms coming from the USA and USSR stimulating; their authors put forward theories which were too simplistic for his taste. One of them was **Jerome Bruner**.

It's incredible that representatives of large countries who want to change the world, have no other ambition about a subject than to construct an adaptable language and images which conform to a model.

Is intelligence merely representation or is it essentially invention? The pre-eminence that these authors give to images makes for a conservative model of intelligence.

I believe, on the other hand, that activity consists of modifying reality and not of imitating it. Sputniks wouldn't be built or journeys to the moon planned from simply observing and repeating information.

It's inconceivable that creative spirits can be worried by the idea that each child has the capacity to invent and re-invent. If this is how teachers of the old school thought, well, so be it. But, then...

I must say that at the end of a career, it's better to be prepared to change perspective, rather than be condemned simply to repeating things.

Perhaps being a citizen of a small country like Switzerland in the end had advantages: he felt less inclined to pontificate.

How does one pass from a stage of lesser knowledge to that of greater understanding?

What is happening inside the perceptive individual?

Rigorous thought.

How does human knowledge evolve?

'Transitional' psychologist in search of epistemological answers.

A child psychologist recognised and praised throughout the world.

I need to build a theoretical-scientific model that will be understandable.

- In empirical research and written theory, Piaget considered the basic problems and concepts again and again.

- In his scientific work, it is difficult to find definitive answers to the questions posed. Searching for the truth which he never considered to be absolute, he tirelessly pursued the understanding of those creative links through which human beings acquire knowledge.

- In the process of building genetic psychology, as in any scientific discipline, his aim and his methods were defined...

What is the aim?

The object of genetic psychology is the thinking individual (epistemological). Piaget is interested in:

- the common **cognitive structures** that appear at a particular stage of development, and

- the **process of formation** of such structures, their **psychogenesis**, in normal individuals.

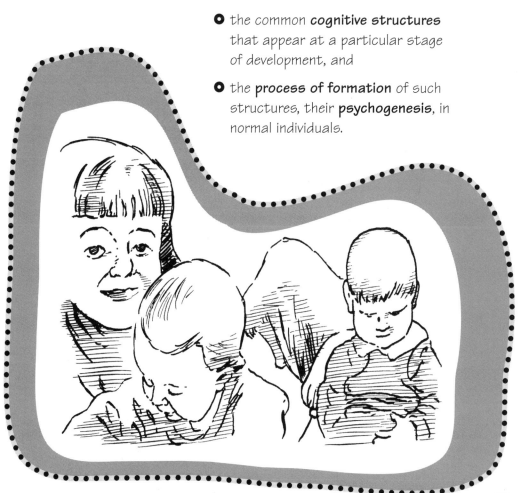

Child psychology has the aim of studying integrated development (intellectual, emotional, social etc.) as well as individual variation.

Genetic psychology is interested in the development the individual achieves in making sense of the world from birth to adolescence, when, ideally, the logical structures of thought are established.

Piaget is not unaware that knowledge has its source in society and that emotional life is its fuel, but he centred his epistemological interest on the investigation of the individual's own potential for building knowledge. He leaves the way open for others to research the social construction of knowledge.

Other differences would become apparent...

Evolutionary psychology is descriptive

'A two year old makes taller towers than a baby of eighteen months. He uses both the vertical and the horizontal, even combining the two. In the realm of larger motor functions, he can go up stairs, climb and kick.'

The social behaviour of children is described in all areas of expression. Each stage of evolution is described and categorised in a linear way.

Genetic psychology is explanatory

'From two years onwards a series of pre-logical behaviours can be observed, the precursors of what will become the functions of serialisation, classification, etc...'

Genetic psychology makes the non-observable intelligible in the youngest children, discovering the systems or structures which explain it. In this way, stages are determined (as will be seen later on) in the evolution of these systems.

What interests Piaget is the order in which this evolution actually happens and not the description of what should happen at each age.

11 A question of method

① What is the most appropriate method to research cognitive processes?
① How do we get to know what children are interested in, and the way in which they explore or develop those interests?

Genetic psychology could have used the classic methods of psychology, such as tests or observation. However...

BINET'S LABORATORY

Piaget applying a psychometric test

What do you see here?

Fixed sequences of questions that we put to each child in an identical way don't take into account what interests each one of them. Moreover, they are leading questions prompting certain responses and they measure diligence rather than the potential competence of the individual...

Piaget uses the pure method of observation with his young children.

SCENE 1

Flossie doesn't love me because I told her to have a nap.

SCENE 2

Pipo and I are going shopping. You stay here, Flossie, because you've got to have a nap.

Noooo!

Observing children presents difficulties: one of these is that they have conversations amongst themselves which are very tied in with action. To the expert eye, Scene 1 differs from Scene 2 by the type of thinking which is being used. However, the difference is very subtle...

So, how does one really distinguish one type of thinking from another, by just observing?

Piaget had already proved that if he intervened...

It's obvious that in terms of Piaget's epistemological interests, using psychometric tests and pure observation doesn't serve the purpose. The methods have to be adaptable to the particular theoretical problems which are presented.

The clinical method

If there's a method that's indissolubly linked to genetic psychology, as well as its central theoretical concepts, it's the **clinical method**.

As other methods did not allow for total involvement with the object, Piaget and his collaborators adopted the clinical method for their research. Originating in psychiatry, in this new field the method underwent a process of adjustment and revision, as one can see in Piaget's biography. Due to its complexity an interviewer needs at least two years' training in order to use it.

THE INTERVIEWER:

- has a chosen hypothesis to confirm or reject;

- directs the conversation and at the same time is led by the replies of the subject (to provoke and be provoked);

- observes, intervenes or keeps quiet at the appropriate time;

- tries not to lose the thread, or end the conversation, or let it take unpredictable paths.

INTERVIEWEES:

- must try to express themselves freely, without prompting;

- are asked to go over their assertions several times.

In applying the clinical method, everything is subject to criticism: the theory in relation to practice, the interventions of the interviewer in relation to the questions formulated...

It's called the clinical method of research when it is focused on exploring the child's beliefs.

For example, a researcher starts from the following questions:

- ⊕ what meaning does a child give to the origin of life? and
- ⊕ how does the child assimilate ideas that come from science and religion into his thought?

Ariel, 7 years old, goes to a state school in the morning and in the afternoon to a religious one.

Lilian is the interviewer. She has a preliminary supposition: Ariel is going to have a conflict between the religious and the basic scientific information that he possesses.

What is the origin of life?

What does 'origin' mean?

Lilian could have asked if this always happens. Would Ariel sustain this hypothesis, by which he would have to admit that he himself had been an orangutan? However, she decides to follow another path of investigation: **the religious version**.

And why do some people come from Adam and Eve?

Because they got married and had lots of children.

And where did animals come from?

The teacher says they come from water, like the dinosaurs, but now they have shrunk, some have grown wings and others live in the rocks.

And has the mess on the earth been tidied up?

Yes, because God has made it tidy.

Ariel goes back to combining the religious and the scientific explanations. He opts for the first version without needing to amend the second.

(*) the conversation recreated here is an example quoted and analysed in 'Genetic Psychology. Methodological aspects and pedagogic implications', compiled by Miño and Dávila publications.

The clinical method is not the only one used in genetic psychology. Together with **structural** and **psychogenetic** methods, it forms part of the nucleus of Piagetian theory. One can easily see that the three methods adapt themselves well to the central epistemological problems.

Clinical method investigates the intellectual system of each child through directed questioning.

Structural analysis, in order to systematise stages, tries to reconstruct in a research environment the cognitive system which underlies the information provided by children

The psychogenetic method reconstructs the history through which the cognitive systems have evolved.

The structural method

The urge to explain reality, rather than being content with merely describing it, gives Jean Piaget's epistemology its scientific character.

Through structural analysis, Piaget tries to understand the seemingly random in children's behaviour to determine the underlying (invisible) structures which explain it. Gestalt sets out for the first time the concept of structure in psychology: the whole is made up of a system of relationships. The whole cannot be reduced to each element taken independently.

WHAT DO THESE CHILDREN'S REPLIES HAVE IN COMMON?

Using structural method, these different reactions are 'read' as an expression of the child's way of interpreting the world at a particular moment in the development of his intelligence.

These children have not yet acquired the concept of number. Amongst other things, this is because they do not recognise one of its properties: equivalence between groups. They can, however, recognise equivalence when there is a spatial correspondence between the elements of one group or another. This is the beginning of the formation of a complex concept like that of number.

Until Piaget, the stage before achieving intellectual operations was considered obscure and defined as a lack or an error. His contribution was to give a positive meaning to these beginnings. Only through these can the beginnings be reconstructed.

Gestalt would say that it is a problem of perception...

This is partly true. We gradually diminish our perceptive vision, thanks to a mechanism which regulates perception. However, illusion doesn't totally disappear. Sometimes, certain features tend to deform the object. Our perception is deceptive.

If you cover up the top of the picture on the left, can you see the birds in the drawing?

The strings are equal; this one's extra bit is the bit missing there... And you didn't cut it or add anything.

The boy can infer that, apart from the visual differences he perceives, nothing was added or taken away and thus the quantity remains unchanged.

Structural analysis also permits the study of how one system of knowledge gives way to another, more evolved, one. This supposes that every system that is reached has been preceded by others from which it has inherited certain elements. The oldest structure is thus recognised as having a positive character. Until Piaget, the children in the previous examples, insofar as they failed to grasp the concept, would have been said to have committed an 'error'. This would have made it harder to understand how this concept comes into being. Piaget, however, tries to characterise this behaviour in depth, investigating the structure which maintains it.

In order for the description of structures and systems of structures which underlie this behaviour to be formally and rigorously presented, Piaget uses the conceptualisation of another doctrine: logic.

The culmination of structural analysis lies in the explanation of the systems which underlie child behaviour through a mathematical logical model.

The psychogenetic method reconstructs the process by which the structures of knowledge are formed. It tries to explain how the subjects create rules which allow them to understand reality. By this route, psychogenesis allows us to reconstruct scientific knowledge.

What are the laws of change
from one system to another?

What are the factors
that influence change?

THE PSYCHOGENETIC METHOD...

does not concern itself
with structures.

does concern itself with the
mechanics of the formation
of structures.

Every system of knowledge evolves from others and opens up the possibility of new systems which emerge from a reorganisation of the previous one.

GENESIS → DIALECTICAL RELATIONSHIP → STRUCTURE

Now I understand why it isn't just one more example of evolutionary psychology.

Before, one spoke of the transforming action of the subject. Now, the genesis-structure dialectic presents itself... Mmm....I would have been interested in knowing the principles of this theory!

Marx was unable to. Let's explore it...

12 There is no genesis without structure and vice versa

According to Gestalt, structures are 'givens' in the field of perception and there is no way of grasping their origins. Structures change, but they do so through 'insight', which is a sudden reorganisation of the field of perception.

For genetic psychology, structures must be understood in terms of their origins. At the same time, the origin has meaning in respect of a previous structure and of a subsequent one.

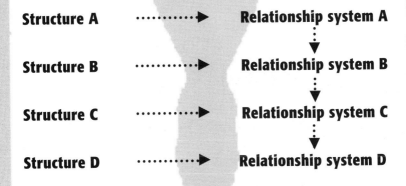

Structure A ············▶ **Relationship system A**

Structure B ············▶ **Relationship system B**

Structure C ············▶ **Relationship system C**

Structure D ············▶ **Relationship system D**

The **psychogenetic method** investigates the mechanism which leads to the transformation of one system into another.

...as much
with life
as with
knowledge

Evolution. A philosophical idea which attempts to explain the dynamic, changing nature of things during the passing of time. Simple forms of life, or poorly adjusted ones, are likely to change in stages in order to acquire forms which are more complex and, in particular, better adapted.

For the body:
end of growth, maturity
of the organs.

**For the life of
the mind:**
adult mind

**For emotional life and
social relationships:**
a balance of feelings.

For intelligence:
systematisation of
adult reason.

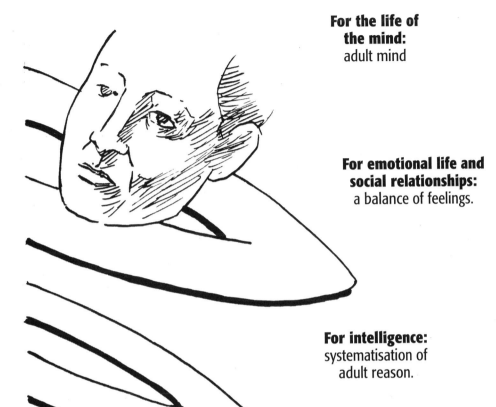

Psychological development, which
begins at birth and continues
throughout adulthood, is comparable to organic growth: like the
latter, it essentially consists of a
move towards balance: from the
instability of childhood ideas
towards the systematisation of
adult reason. It is clear that in
the case of human knowledge,
these features acquire special
characteristics.

ORGANIC GROWTH	MENTAL DEVELOPMENT
static (reaches a maxi- mum point)	**mobile** (the more stable, the more mobile)
unstable regressive evolution	**tendency to equilibrium** limitless progress (for a healthy mind)

mobile equilibrium

Mental evolution is like assembling a subtle mechanism in whose gradual adjustment the pieces become lighter and more mobile. And in this mobility resides the stability of its balance.

14 How does a child learn?

TEST OF PRECONCEPTIONS ABOUT LEARNING

Tick where appropriate

1. Through daily contact with people and objects. ☐

2. Through teaching by adults. ☐

3. Through sanctions for what it does badly and stimulus from what it does well. ☐

4. Add anything else you can think of.......................................
....
....

Result

▷ If you ticked points 1, 2, 3, you tend to think that:
  – Learning is a process directed from outside.

Your conceptualisation of learning coincides with that of conductivism.

▷ If you ticked any of points 1, 2, 3 and also completed item 4 with some sentence of this kind:
  – 'In an autoconstructive process';
  – 'In the interaction with its environment';
  – 'In the transforming action of objects';

then

Your conceptualisation of learning coincides with that of Piagetian constructivism.

Knowledge is constructed (functional Piaget)

Piaget assumes that the organism must necessarily be located in an environment and that it cannot live or develop outside it. But what he is interested in discovering is:

**WHAT HAPPENS WITHIN THE SUBJECT
WHEN LEARNING TAKES PLACE?**

To answer this, Piaget introduces and emphasises an explanatory factor which permits the understanding of learning itself, from the psychological perspective:

Man is a being with the capacity to construct himself.

The external conditions in which knowledge is produced interest me much less, because such knowledge is a product of the activity of the subject and not the pressure of reality.

Let's go a little further into the constructivist theory of knowledge.

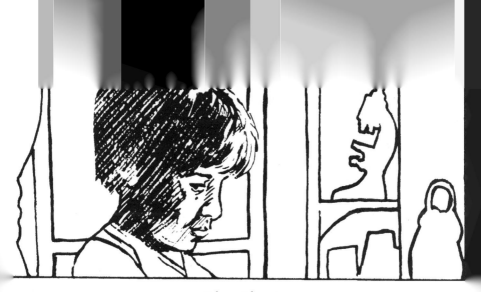

It is not innate.

It does not originate in the environment.

Subject and object are indivisible. They form each other.

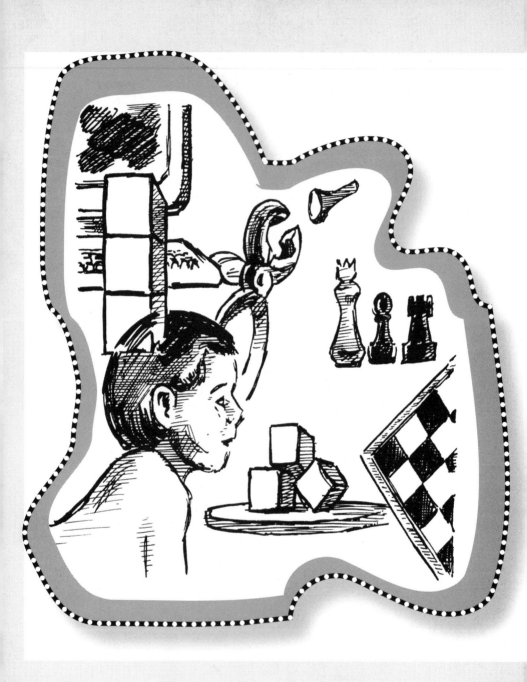

The presence of an active subject who in that interaction increases personal understanding of the world is necessary in order for evolved knowledge to grow.

During the first moments of life, there is no difference between the 'I' and the world of the baby. There is no 'I'. There is no such world.

At about one year, the baby can perceive itself as independent from its mother.

In this theory of knowledge, is 'action' the same as 'movement'?

An action is:
a movement directed towards external objects, or objects internal to the subject, with some intentionality, especially that of giving meaning to the object.

An action is not:
a simple movement of the body which does not generate knowledge, which transforms neither subject nor object.

An action can be: material, (product of a motor activity);

mental, (a perception, the relationship between concepts etc.).

I don't believe that the object is transformed because someone knows it...

The object is transformed as an 'object of knowledge' when new properties which define it can be assigned to it.

Intelligence organises the world... and itself

For Piaget, intelligence begins neither with the knowledge of self nor of things in themselves. It begins with the interaction between the subject and the object as they orient themselves simultaneously towards the two poles of this interaction.

Let us take as an example the first two months of life:

From the beginning, babies develop actions. Very soon, these start to become co-ordinated. Co-ordinated, they form systems. In genetic psychology these are called **schemas of action**.

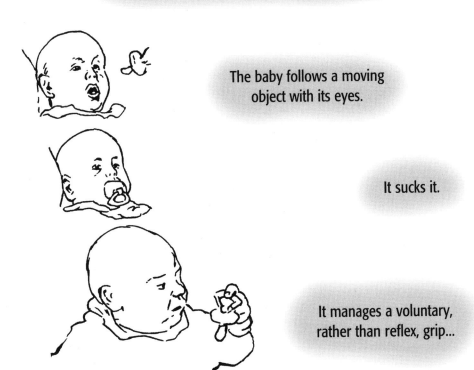

A schema is a succession of actions, either material or internalised, which have an organisation and which are susceptible to repetition in similar circumstances.

The baby follows a moving object with its eyes.

It sucks it.

It manages a voluntary, rather than reflex, grip...

In principle, these schemas of action are isolated, they are not co-ordinated. Nobody guarantees that for the baby the object it sucks and the one it grasps will be the same object. Looking, sucking and grasping are, for him, different kinds of knowledge.

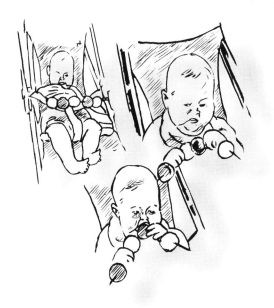

At 4-5 months, the schemas co-ordinate and an object can be observable, agreeable and at the same time suckable. It will give rise to a new schema.

Through the schemas of action a primitive classification of the world is achieved, according to certain qualities: what can be looked at, grasped, sucked, etc.

Does the baby have an idea of this classification?

No, the baby only 'thinks' in actions. Objects only exists for it in so far as it can act on them (in this case, see, touch, suck). The possibility of attributing properties to objects depends on the action of the subject.

If the eyes don't see, the object doesn't exist

In its interchanges with the world, the child begins to place itself in a world which slowly begins to objectify and to organise itself.

Piaget studied his own children in their formative years. He showed that there are concepts which, contrary to what has been seen as common sense, take many years to become definitively established. Such is the case with the permanence of the object.

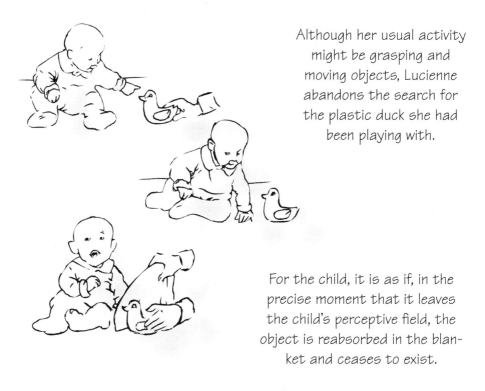

Although her usual activity might be grasping and moving objects, Lucienne abandons the search for the plastic duck she had been playing with.

For the child, it is as if, in the precise moment that it leaves the child's perceptive field, the object is reabsorbed in the blanket and ceases to exist.

Thanks to the co-ordination and differentiation of the schemas, the object can acquire a substantive permanence, which guarantees its 'objective' existence beyond the action of the subject.

When does knowledge begin?

There is no exact time. It is at the moment that hereditary reflexes begin to function in relation to the external world.

Until Piaget, psychology maintained that symbolic function begins with language.

There are reflexes which remain identical although they disappear and reappear. For example, the walking reflex, present at birth, which will only reappear at around one year of age when, thanks to complex co-ordination, the child does actually manage to walk.

For a conductivist psychologist, what we have here is a combination of reflexes made more complex by the conditioning which external stimuli produce.

For a psychogeneticist, it's about a being who is going out to conquer the world with action, broadening the field in which the reflex is applied.

There are reflexes which change and give rise to schemas of action.

The baby can, eventually, grasp what it sees, follow with its eyes what it hears, etc., an ability that is not present at first.

This operation sets in motion the initial abilities of the new born, enabling it to construct variable forms.

The constant is that these always have as their function the facilitation of the organism to adapt to its environment.

A basic principle of biology is that every species, every organism, organises itself and adapts to its environment.

Then where can one find the biological basis of the theory of knowledge?

◎ In the first reflex actions, which give rise to the birth of intelligence in the child, and especially...
◎ in the tendency to organise knowledge in structures which are progressively more related to reality;
◎ and in the mechanism of adaptation to the environment, as a product of the activities of assimilation and adaptation.

Intelligence is, in principle, that capacity to adapt to new situations. Then comes creation, invention. Isn't life itself a continuous creation of ever more complex forms? Isn't it a progressive equilibrium between these forms and the environment? Intelligence is a particular case of biological adaptation to the environment. I am supposing, in saying this, that it is an organisation and that its function is to structure the universe.

In the same way, a mollusc, a willow, a stomach or any living organism or system, structures and restructures itself in relation to its immediate environment.

Put the following words into the right order:

ASSIMILATION   ACCOMMODATION   ADAPTATION

 Small as a pinhead, the amoeba, a unicellular animal, can live in the muddy bottoms of ponds.

Moving one part and then another, it goes in search of nutritious particles.

 As it lengthens one part of itself, it traps the particle and incorporates it into its body.

The body of the amoeba trans-forms the particle into new compo-nents. These go on to form part of the substance of the amoebic cell.

 The amoeba detaches itself from that for which it has no use and, leaving it behind, goes in search of more food.

ADAPTATION
= interplay between:

ASSIMILATION   **ACCOMMODATION**

Conclusion
- The amoeba is adapted to the environment in which it lives (adaptation).
- The amoeba's circumstances (the particles it can consume, the environment in which it finds itself) determine its form and structure (accommodation).
- The type of food chosen is in its turn determined by the characteristics of the amoeba (assimilation).

Our intellectual structure can be conceived of as abstract organs of adaptation. These structures are based, throughout their development, on processes similar to those which rule the functioning and evolution of any living being.

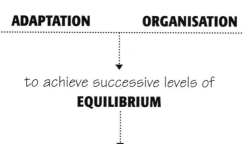

ADAPTATION   **ORGANISATION**

to achieve successive levels of
EQUILIBRIUM

This form of functioning of the organism in relation to its environment:

- is innate;
- is common to all living beings;
- is necessary;
- moulds the subject throughout its development.

The development of intelligence is ruled by the same mechanisms as other biological processes.

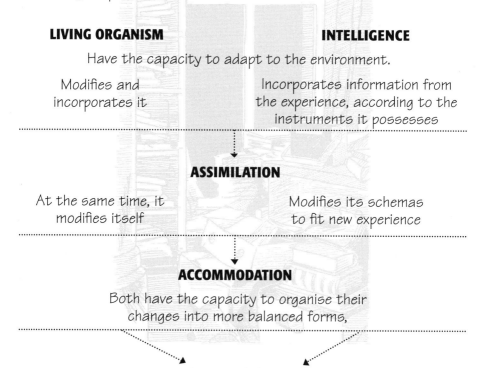

LIVING ORGANISM   **INTELLIGENCE**

Have the capacity to adapt to the environment.

Modifies and   Incorporates information from
incorporates it   the experience, according to the
                                   instruments it possesses

ASSIMILATION

At the same time, it   Modifies its schemas
modifies itself   to fit new experience

ACCOMMODATION

Both have the capacity to organise their
changes into more balanced forms,

respond to purely internal motives.

Experience is important at any point in the acquisition of knowledge, but only if it is assimilated and interpreted by the system which the subject possesses to give it meaning.

Piaget uses the following example to make graphic the mechanism of assimilation:

A rabbit, like any organism, feeds on substances. It incorporates them, giving them its own structure.

Knowledge is structured within the subject (knowledge is not a simple copy).

◄┈┈┈┈ ASSIMILATION ┈┈┈►

The rabbit transforms the cabbage into rabbit.

Assimilation: incorporation into the organism of external elements (which have been modified) by the organic or mental structures it possesses for this purpose.

Something is assimilable if, at the same time, it can be incorporated and modified.

For a baby, the world is a reality it can suck...

A spoon, a toy, a blanket... objects are not considered by a baby in terms of their specific differences, but rather in relation to the action that the baby can perform on them. For a baby, all objects are, in principle, suckable.

Objects external to the baby are assimilated to its schemas of action. Thus something can act as a stimulus for it if it can be assimilated by its system.

For an older child, it is a reality to explore with all its senses.

For an adult, it can be a reality to explore and construct using different senses and with different emphases: intellectually, artistically etc.

Schemas of action are the instruments which allow reality to be assimilated; they are continually being modified. For this reason, genetic psychology also calls them assimilation schemas.

In the case of intelligence, it is not simply a case of physiological assimilation, but of meaningful assimilation. Through this, the subject is able to attribute new meanings, make new syntheses.

In summary: Piaget distinguishes two complementary aspects of the origins of knowledge in its journey towards equilibrium:

1 Unchanging structures

The mechanisms which make possible the acquisition of knowledge do not vary. One always knows in the same way. A certain constant functioning exists which ensures the passage from one level to another.

At the level of the functional, it is possible to observe a certain invariability in the processes.

The functional invariables in the building of knowledge are, fundamentally, the mechanisms of adaptation: assimilation and accommodation.

Each one of these functions takes place in a distinct way, depending on the level one is dealing with.

2 Variable structures

These represent successive states of equilibrium which mark the differences between the basic behaviour of the new born and the behaviour of the adolescent.

Genetic psychology determines the following successive stages which are characterised by the appearance of these structures:

sensorimotor;
preoperational;
concrete operations;
formal operations.

And people? What do they know? What do they acquire knowledge of?

1. of the world, of reality.
2. of general categories or forms which organise this knowledge.

I was the first to maintain the need for categories or forms which organise and give meaning to knowledge about the world. Without them, knowledge would be chaotic. There are ideas which are innate and necessary.

KANT

1724-1804

I agree on that point. However, you will know that I tried to go beyond the explanation based on the innateness of these forms by investigating their origin. It is absolutely clear that they are all products of the construction of a working organism.

Piaget explains these forms as structures. He also considers them necessary. For him, however, they go beyond any hereditary preformation. They come from the transforming action of the subject on the environment. They can thereby discover its properties.

15 Structural Piaget

As a revolutionary theorist, Piaget questions the most obvious: that which previously is undisputed, that which, lacking a theoretical system to sustain it, is unacknowledged.

Such is the case with his investigation into the acquisition of the notions of self preservation.

BEWARE OF 'ADULTOMORPHISM'

It's lucky that they've spread out like that. It makes the audience look larger...

The actor knows that his perception is deceptive. At this performance, the audience is small.

For an adult, it is logically evident that, however the elements of a group are distributed in space, its number is unchanging. A child under 6 or 7 would probably not share this opinion.

How does genetic psychology explain this phenomenon? Piaget is careful not to attribute adult ways of understanding the world to children (adultomorphism). Otherwise, he would be saying 'the children are wrong'.

In his research into the development of knowledge from birth, he avoids falling into the trap of adultomorphism.

Experiments on the idea of conservation

1. Conservation of matter (experiment with solids)

Are these pieces of dough equal?

Yes.

We're going to pretend that these are little rolls. If one little boy ate this one and another little boy ate the other, would they both eat the same amount of bread, or would one have eaten more than the other?

Yes, of course. The same.

And if I turn one of the rolls into a French stick and leave the other one as it is, which boy would eat more? Or would they eat the same amount?

The one who ate the French stick.

Why?

Because it's longer.

There's more to eat on this one

Ah...And if I turn this roll into breadcrumbs and leave this one, is there the same amount to eat on both plates or is there more on one of them?

Every transformation of the object signifies for the child a change relative to the quantity of the material substance.

2. Conservation of quantity (experiment with liquids)

The same reasoning is established experimenting with liquids. For the child there is a greater or smaller quantity, according to the container in which the liquid is placed. This sets one property above the other. For example, width is a sign that 'there is more' than in a taller container, or the other way round.

However, at about 6 or 7 years it begins to be evident to the child that the amount of the substance cannot vary.

The amount of bread is the same. The French stick is longer, but thinner than the round roll.

Why are they equal?
Because although the dimensions of the object have varied, these variations are mutually compensated for.

You didn't add anything or take anything away!

Why are they equal?
Because nothing has been added or taken away.

If you knead the French stick again, it will turn into a round roll again.

Why are they equal?
Because it is possible to return to the original state.

Conservation experiment II: the horizontal nature of the surface of liquids.

Everyday life presents numerous situations in which it can be observed that, regardless of the container in which the liquid is placed, the surface maintains the horizontal. However, for a child of under 6 or 7, this does not constitute 'evidence of perception'.

Contrary to what common sense suggests, sight is not a sufficient instrument to sustain the preservation of the liquid's horizontal nature. Only when the child can take a point of reference external to the container will it be able to solve this problem. And this implies a series of complex co-ordinations which will always go beyond simple perception.

At about 4 years old, water is a circular stain within the bottle. The level of the surface is not represented, although the child can observe it and for some time has been able to draw straight lines as well.

Between 5 and 7 years old, the child identifies the parallels between the bottom and the surface. but transfers this property to any position the bottle is in.

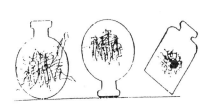

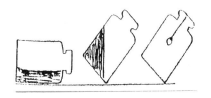

Conclusion: without the experiment, the child would not manage to establish the permanence of the horizontal nature of liquids. However, the acquisition of this knowledge cannot be explained solely by the experiment alone.

In his studies on the origins of the notion of conservation, Piaget shows that:

1. Up to 6 or 7 years, faced with a deformed object, children assert, in their own way, that neither its weight, nor its volume, nor the material itself is conserved.
2. At about 6 or 7, they begin to maintain that the material itself does not change.

Between 1 and 2 above, children go through a period of transition in which they sometimes assert and sometimes deny that things are conserved, depending on the conditions of the experiment.

The conservation of the material itself is the first kind of understanding of conservation that the child achieves in relation to the physical properties of objects.

The 'million dollar question' is: how is this movement from the non-permanence of the quantity of the substance to the assertion of the exact opposite, to an idea better adapted to reality, possible? What are the factors responsible for this evolution?

You will ask 'How is this movement from stupidity to wisdom possible?'

It is not correct to understand it in this way. What children respond to in any one case are ideas consistent with the respective systems of thinking. They are ideas which exist of necessity. When the supposed errors of children are systematic, repeated, there is an opportunity to discover the 'logic' which underlies them. Of course, only the adult is able to understand this logic, not the child...

And why not believe that a child's knowledge is attributable to what it has learned from adults?

Lets see... would it occur to us to teach a child that when a loaf is changed into breadcrumbs, the quantity of food doesn't change? Perhaps. But even so, we would be left unable to explain why little children assert that the quantity is not preserved. Where do they get that from? You're not going to tell me that it's the product of teaching!

I don't think that's true of my daughter. She already talks about atoms and molecules!

Sugar is formed by atoms. When you put it in water, the atoms separate.

You can't see the sugar in this glass any more. Where is it?

The atoms have disappeared; they have become water. They don't take up any space any more...

Until about 11 years, children cannot grasp the concept of the material being constant even when it changes its state between liquid and solid.

I know! It must have something to do with maturing at a certain age...

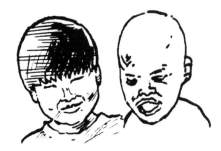

No, no... We have proved that in every culture the appearance of this notion happens at different ages. This means that the social environment can speed up or delay its appearance.

Great! The notion of conservation is not attributable to teaching. Nor does it happen at a particular age... So what is your 'scientific' revelation?

Calm down! What remains constant in each case is the sequence of particular behaviours. What does not change is the order in which they appear. For example, children, like pre-Socratic philosophers, first assert the conservation of matter. Only later do they accept the conservation of weight and volume.

How can they believe that something goes on being what it was, having the same quantity of material, and at the same time assert that its weight or volume has changed?

Even before the child is able to weigh or measure, it asserts that the object as such continues to exist, as long as nothing has been taken away or added... He affirms the substance as if it were an empty shape. But remember that he can't reach that conclusion just through the perception of the object; the facts of the experiment are not sufficient.

That means that when the child asserts the conservation of the substance as an unchanging quality of the physical object, he does so despite the fact that other properties, like form or appearance, vary...

Yes! He does so on a strictly logical basis. And the proof is in the children's replies.

Why isn't there the same quantity, if you didn't take out or put in anything? What a question! What are you trying to prove? It's obvious! Do you think I'm stupid?

It seems impossible that he himself thought the exact opposite a little while ago; he doesn't even doubt or need to prove what he's saying.

When an understanding of conservation arises, it does so with the force of evidence.

Three theoretical principles for a theory of knowledge

Constructivism

Subjects interact with reality, building up their knowledge and, at the same time, their own minds. Knowledge is never a copy of reality; it is always a construction.

Realism

The object of knowledge is not identified with reality. Reality exists independently, whether or not it is known by anyone, and in addition, cannot be known directly.

Through their cognitive structuring activity, the subjects delineate knowable zones, thus establishing their own objects of knowledge.

Interactionism

The possibility of establishing oneself depends on one's ability to develop different activities in the world. The object is constructed as the subject establishes a dialectical relationship between both of them.

If the point of departure is the action of the subject on the world, we can say that we are faced with a constructive interaction. The subject interacts with the object, constructing new meanings of a reality the existence of which is assumed (realism).

Four factors for mental development

1 Organic growth and maturing

Organic maturing, which constitutes a necessary condition for new behaviour to appear, is not sufficient in itself. Research has shown that it must be accompanied by functional exercise and many experiments.

Although it has not yet been possible to be precise about what conditions of maturity are needed for the appearance of major operating structures, it is known that maturity has less and less importance as age increases. By contrast, the influence of the physical and social environment grows in importance.

The further away the early years (a 'sensorimotor' period, as we shall see later on), the less predictable the moment at which the acquisitions make their appearance. The chronology varies, not the order in which they occur.

To summarise: organic maturing, although it does not in itself explain mental development, constitutes an indispensable factor, insofar as it allows an unchanging order of a succession of stages.

2 Interaction and social transmission

Interaction and social transmissions, including school learning, are situations into which the individual puts energy and receives something in exchange.

It might be thought that, in learning situations in which the child has a passive role, merely as receptor, genetic psychology holds that if learning did take place, it is because of an action of assimilation. This is a condition of learning.

What place, then, does affectivity (the ability to feel emotions) have in the development of the subject? Piaget makes it clear that affectivity is the energising force of any conduct, however intellectual it may be.

The mobilising force of cognitive development is always affective and, inversely, there could not be affective states without perception and knowledge. The two factors, cognitive and affective, are constituents of evolution. It would be useless to reduce one to the other.

3 Exercise and experience

Mental development is produced in the experience of interaction of the subject with the objects of knowledge. Exercise and experience with objects and one's own actions are essential.

4 Equilibrium

How are three such disparate factors as these organised in the construction of orderly progressive structures?

Piaget does not believe in a pre-established plan or one which can only be understood by reference to an adult model. In the child one can prove a progressive, uninterrupted construction such that every motivation takes place only with reference to the preceding ones. The internal mechanism of this process is equilibration, which represents a series of active compensations on the part of the subject in response to external disruption.

From the beginning of life, action in the world works to produce progressive balances of accommodation and assimilation. This results in a kind of adaptation by the intelligence to new situations and, at the same time, demonstrates its tendency towards organisation.

Whenever there is knowledge, this functional mechanism comes into play and these are its laws.

16 Here comes 'the man of stages'

Piaget, who was always alert to any change in the progress of scientific thought, disdained technological progress in his own daily life. He almost never watched television, rarely went to the cinema and only drove a car for a few years. It was common to see him arriving at the university on a bicycle, under the reproving glance of some colleague.

Piaget would never hesitate to define himself as a scientific epistemologist.

For philosophers, he is an aberrant philosopher, because he tries to verify by scientific experiment a subject traditionally reserved for philosophical speculation.

For psychologists and educators, Piaget is the man of stages. As the most functional aspects of psychogenetic theory (that is to say those which explain the mechanism by which one knows) developed, the notion of stages became significant again and to some extent, the theory itself became less interesting.

Perhaps because it is the simplest to convey, the theory of stages of intellectual evolution make Jean Piaget famous.

What is a 'stage'?

Cognitive development is constructive, not linear, and goes through different moments. Piaget calls these successive organisations, which have a certain level of stability and which imply new cognitive conquests, 'stages'. Each one of them is characterised by a particular structure.

Another more functional way of conceiving of stages is to characterise them as different ways which the subject has to tackle problems. They would therefore be common forms of organising reality, of demonstrating one's ability in different fields: motor, intellectual, affective.

The sequence in which the progress of intelligence happens is always the same; what varies is the age at which the structures appear. This depends on various factors, amongst which are the subject's personal history and his environment.

Each stage appears, defined by a structure. These are not observable; what is seen are the different behaviours which these structures manifest.

Intelligence is the form of equilibrium towards which all structures aim. Its formation can be understood by the most basic sensorimotor mechanisms.

Each structure is a particular form of equilibrium: in its own sphere, more or less stable, but at the limits of this, more susceptible to being unstable.

Each structure is followed by another according to an evolutionary law: each one ensures a broader and more stable equilibrium for the processes which are central to the preceding one.

Functional continuity, co-ordinated with structural differentiation, defines a development sequence.

The sensorimotor stage (0-2 years)

The period which stretches between birth and the acquisition of language is marked by extraordinary mental development, incomparable to that at any other moment of life.

Since thought cannot be expressed in words until there is representation, thought is manifested in acts. Acts are related to the present, as there is no representation. When this does make its appearance, the next stage starts.

Piaget says that in this first stage of life, there is a real...

Copernican revolution

In two years, through perception and movement, the child conquers the practical universe which surrounds it. From a state of inability to distinguish between itself and the world, in which the new-born refers everything to its own body, the child becomes one more amongst others in the universe which it has constructed and which is exterior to itself.

In this process three phases can be distinguished:

- that of the reflexes;
- that of the organisation of repeated perceptions;
- that of sensorimotor intelligence itself.

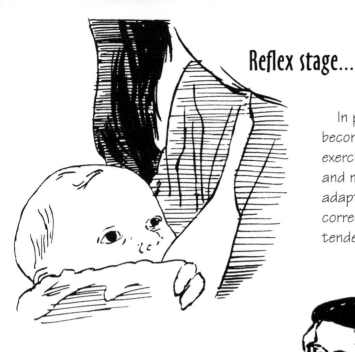

Reflex stage...

In principle, mental life becomes apparent in reflex exercises which are sensory and motor co-ordinations, adapted by heredity. They correspond to instinctive tendencies like nutrition.

If it's all instinct, then it's all the same...

No, not at all!. We already saw that the child develops a real activity. Think: the sucking action becomes refined through exercise; as the days pass, the new born sucks better, it acquires practical knowledge of the situation.

Later, a generalisation of the activities of sucking happens: sucking its hand and sucking anything that comes to its mouth. That is to say that the new born assimilates a part of its universe through sucking. For this reason, its activity is known as 'sensorimotor assimilation'.

The organisation of perceptions and habits stage...

Experience enables the baby to start to co-ordinate schemas of action: the thumb is systematically sucked; the baby turns its head to follow an object which interests it, smiles at the human face, etc.

The practical or sensorimotor intelligence stage...

This is an intelligence which is not based on symbols or words, but on the manipulation of objects. It has, as tools, perceptions and movements organised in schemas of action.

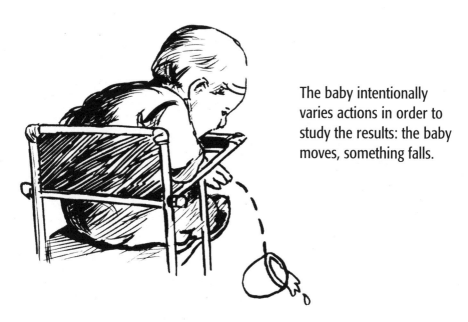

The baby intentionally varies actions in order to study the results: the baby moves, something falls.

Schemas of action are co-ordinated and multiply through new experimental behaviours. Later on, in the same way, concepts become co-ordinated.

The baby, faced with a new object, incorporates it into each of its schemas of action in order to understand it.

When an action is repeated and generalised in new situations, it is correct to define it as a sensorimotor concept.

An example of sensorimotor thought, of internalised action, is that of Martina at 16 months.

Martina wants to take the pebble out of the matchbox, but the gap is too small for her fingers.

It can be inferred that the baby created in her mind a sensorimotor representation of the implicit in this problem. This acts as a model or mental schema which then...

...can be transferred to the concrete situation. This is a culminating moment in the development of her intelligence.

Through mental representation, the little girl has invented new methods of activity.

Throughout this phase, thanks to the constructive activity of the child, objects little by little start to acquire permanence. That is to say they have their own existence and stop being mere extensions of the self.

In addition, the child begins to establish cause/effect relationships between actions. When it cries, its mother comes. When it pulls a string at the end of which is the object it wants, this comes near. When it opens a box, music sounds.

What are the limitations of thought at this stage?

Thought is contained within its own sensorimotor register. For this reason, one speaks of the egocentrism of this first manifestation of intelligence. The child knows certain properties of objects, but

- not beyond where his action leads it and,
- the child can't explain why the objects behave as they do.

The preoperational stage (2 to 6/7 years)

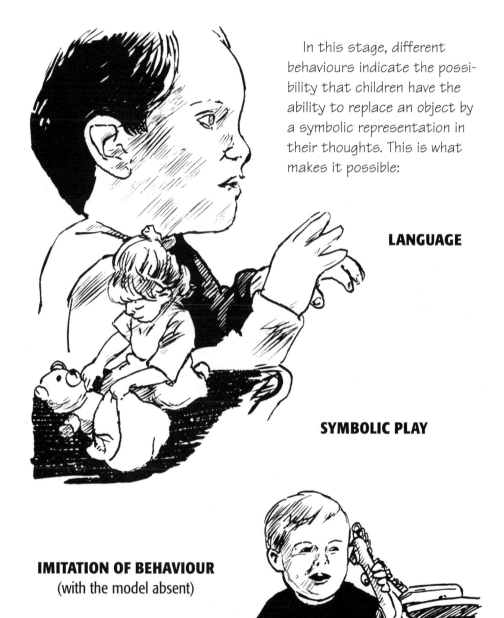

In this stage, different behaviours indicate the possibility that children have the ability to replace an object by a symbolic representation in their thoughts. This is what makes it possible:

LANGUAGE

SYMBOLIC PLAY

IMITATION OF BEHAVIOUR
(with the model absent)

How does this evolution take place?

From sensorimotor representation...

The facts and objects which form part of the baby's world exist within its mental model as a whole. They are replicas or imitations derived from actions which have been carried out with these objects.

For example, a child could have a representation of 'The Mother Object' more or less like this...

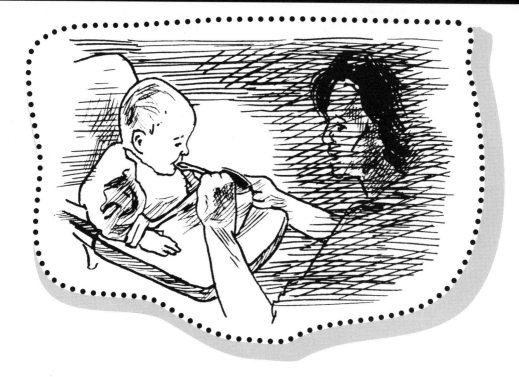

Thomas' representation of his mother is made up of a group of images; feeding, bathtime, being put to bed, getting up, taking walks together...

All these activities have sensory connotations: softness and human warmth, hunger being satisfied, the taste of milk, the smell of soap, her voice, her songs.

The baby recognises his mother's breast
better than her foot because he has had
more direct contact with her breast.

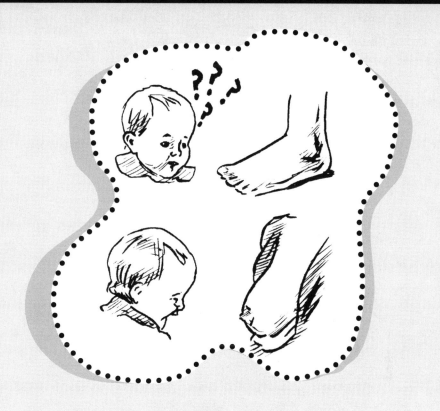

Representation is also made up of spatial qualities: those which he has had the opportunity to explore with sight or touch. Some parts of the figure of his mother will be more defined than others.

Infantile representation of the mother will relate in strength to how well she satisfies his needs. This is the first relationship between intellectual development and affective life.

In the same way, the representation of objects of knowledge which are less meaningful is also the fusion of images of actions carried out with this object.

Sensorimotor representations can be considered as a group of symbols, closely related to the actions which the child can accomplish.

...to preconceptual representation

Julian is playing at feeding his baby elephant. Is it just fun?

Do not disturb
Child thinking

It is really an intense symbolic mental activity, because

1. He uses a previous sensorimotor representation (which he obtained through repeated experiences of eating) in a situation different from that in which it was acquired.

2. He chooses substitute objects (toy bricks are eaten, the toy elephant is he himself, eating) as a basis for his symbolic mental manipulation. He separates his own body from the representation of his behaviour. This can now be applied to external objects.

Sensorimotor thought sensorimotor representations	**Symbolic thought** Symbolic representations
The imitation or internal image is the result of an external activity	The imitation or mental image is recorded, is distanced from the action which gave rise to it. The image can be translated into an activity.

132

Language is a real milestone. At the beginning, language is only a support for action. Children use words to reinforce what they are doing.

The car is going really fast and crashes.

Dalí

Dalí

Dalí

Dalí

Dalí is the name of Alexander's dog. The word 'dog' is a concept, and as such, does not symbolise an individual, but a class of individuals.

For a child who is beginning to talk, this is confusing.

In the first years, children use the same words to indicate an individual or a class of individuals who have certain properties in common. It is for this reason that Piaget calls this symbolic act of the child **preconceptual**.

In the process of construction, substantial changes will take place. Language is used to reconstruct a past action.

The word begins to be a sign, not just a part of the action. The word can evoke the action, although it still does not constitute a symbolic conceptual system.

Why preconcept and not concept?

Because it is still impossible to include the elements in a whole and identify relationships which make up a group.

An example of preconceptual thought:

Lucy (3 years, 2 months and 20 days)

Is that man a daddy?

What is a daddy?

It's a man who has lots of Lucys and Janes.

What are Lucys?

They are little girls and Janes are bigger girls.

Lucy already understands the attribute of the concept of 'daddy'. She knows that it is a class of men who have children. However, to express the concept 'children', she still needs to use specific examples. It is the same when she wants to express the concepts 'little girls' and 'bigger girls'.

Language plays a fundamental role in the development of mental processes. From the private image, children progress towards the public verbal sign.

134

The age of 'why?'

To know how children think spontaneously in this period, there is no more precise method than that of making a list and analysing their questions from when they begin to talk.

At first, the typical question is...

What's that?

From 3 years (or before), any question which adults find difficult to answer will be repeated.

For children, there is no concept of chance in nature, as everything is done for people according to an established and intelligent plan of which the human being is the centre.

The 'why' searches at the same time to investigate the cause and the purpose. In the example above, it would be: what is the reason Berne has no lake? and for what purpose (why?) do they have lakes?

Children in the preoperative or preconceptual period reason with pre-concepts. Preconcepts are half way along the road between the general and the particular.

Luke (4 years, 10 months and 21 days) has a nap every afternoon, but one day he doesn't and says:

We didn't have a nap, so it isn't afternoon.

'Nap' does not imply 'afternoon' for an adult, but for a child it is a possibility. It is a case of prelogical reasoning.

No. That would suppose that logical reasoning is possible at this time. However, it is a prelude to other types of reasoning which will be logical. It would be more appropriate for you to ask yourself 'why do they reason TRANSDUCTIVELY, establishing relationships that are poorly adapted to reality? I'll answer you: because they lack real concepts like 'late'. His elder sister, for example, already knows that....

One would say: that's illogical.

The afternoon begins when I come home, after lunch, when I have my nap. Mum goes out to teach some classes and Dad is in his study...

At this stage, the child will use **juxtaposition** and **syncretism**. Juxtaposition is putting parts together without relating them.

For the child, everything is connected with everything else. In some way, this is like saying 'nothing is connected with anything'. Juxtaposition and syncretism express the way in which children explain the behaviour of things, especially the cause/effect relationship. We'll see an example of this type of thinking: verbal expression.

I went to the zoo. There was a giraffe. We bought popcorn. I fell. The giraffe ate.

Why does the engine go?

Because of the smoke.

What smoke?

The smoke in the tunnel.

For Charles, smoke and movement are juxtaposed as cause and effect, since, from what can be seen of the locomotive, these are the most visible and dynamic signs.

Thought is also reflected in **graphic expression**.

The child thinks that the chain, the pedals and the cogged wheel are necessary for the bicycle to move, but does not know the details of contact and insertion. Juxtaposition, in this case, occurs with the parts of the bicycle.

Syncretic thought creates relationships between all kinds of things. Syncretism is the impossibility of discriminating between parts or between parts and the whole.

Lucy is expressing a syncretic form of understanding the world during the preconceptual stage. It shows an incapacity at that time to relate the parts to the whole.

The preoperational child is also **egocentric**.

Egocentrism is a way of understanding reality in which satisfying the self takes precedence over objective recognition. It is the distortion of reality in order to satisfy the activity and point of view of the subject. Egocentrism is unconscious, the result of a difficulty in distinguishing between the subjective and the objective.

Have you got a little brother?

Yes.

And has your brother got a sister?

No, he doesn't. I am my sister.

Why are you kicking?

Because I don't like the soup. If I kick, it'll get nicer.

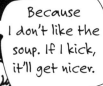

Beneath Zoe's egocentric expressions can be seen a subjective and affective way of understanding the world.

It is clear that egocentric thought is based on an essentially assimilative activity.

Another feature of the preoperational period of thought is **animism**. Animism is the tendency to conceive of things as if they were alive and gifted with intelligence. This also comes from an assimilation of objects into the activity of the child. Everything is exactly the same as the model shown by the self. Thus...

In principle, for a child, any object is alive if it fulfils a role which is useful to the human being. Later on, life is attributed to bodies which can move by themselves.

Language brings with it the possibility of more fluid communication between the child and the other people with whom it comes into contact. In this stage, the child begins to become more institutionalised through education, through which its contacts with its peers become wider. This plays a decisive role in the progress of thought.

The child's ability to explain what he is doing and relating what he has done has the power to transform material behaviour into thought. We have said that, in principle, the child cannot think of a point of view other than his own. Communicating thought and entering into an alien point of view is a slow and difficult learning process.

The first conversations between children are rudimentary and are related to material action. Until they are nearly seven years old, children hardly know how to discuss things among themselves. In reality, they give their own points of view, without thinking about contradictions or coincidences with others.

It's a 'collective monologue'. More than an interchange of thoughts, it is an incitement to action motivated by the fact that it is shared.

It is as if the children were talking to themselves. They are monologues which accompany their games and their action. They make me think of the continual interior dialogue we as adults have.

In the same way that a baby who is still breastfeeding is indifferent to objects, the child of 2 or 3 years is indifferent to other individuals, as is demonstrated by its egocentric language. This will continue evolving until real socialisation is achieved.

Something similar happens with infant play. In a game with rules, the smallest ones play alone, without worrying about the rules of their neighbour.

Between two and seven years, the child's thought evolves in a series of stages. This progress can be described between two poles:

1 From egocentric, totally subjective thought, through pure incorporation or assimilation

2 Towards thought which is adapted to others and in reality, a prelude to logical thought.

There are signs of this evolution in the child's behaviour.

The end of preconcepts

The rectangle is so square... but tiny.

Gemma has formed a primitive concept of 'quadrilateral'. Rectangular or square, even if not defined by the correct properties, they share some which make them belong to the same class.

The end of juxtaposition and syncretism

A bicycle goes on wheels. The man makes them work.

How?

When he drives. He pedals with his legs. That makes the wheels turn round.

What is the chain for?

It's to support the wheels...the pedals, isn't it?

At 6 years, the details and the whole form a related process for Nicholas. However, even if he understands some cause/effect relationships, others still escape him.

The end of egocentrism

It seems as if things are turning, but they've not really.

Sally now does not believe that the world is turning round because she is. She knows it only seems like that.

The concept of conservation is absent in the thinking of the child of 2 to 6 years.

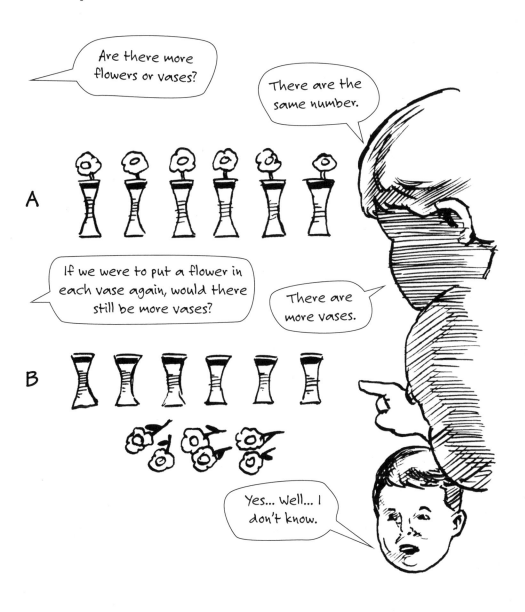

When Alexander is 4 years old, he asserts that in A, there is the same number of flowers and vases. He is sure that in B, there are more vases. A year after this experiment, he has doubts. Before, he either directed his attention to the arrangement of the flowers or to the arrangement of the vases, but not to their mutual relationship. Now, he begins to think in terms of transformation, rather than unconnected states.

What in the sensorimotor period were successive actions or events, each one of them momentary, in the preoperational period, thanks to representation, can be evoked as different moments in an almost simultaneous whole.

Juliet, 5 years old, likes having her name written in front of her.

Go on, write my name! But today you have to write it larger, because yesterday was my birthday.

Juliet still confuses temporal relationships with spatial ones. But although the structure is insufficient, the little girl can give an early form to the organisation of space.

There are always hours, or are there times when there aren't?

Towards the end of this period, children begin to understand that space can be full as well as empty and that there is a lapse of time between these two occurrences.

Mental actions, which produce representations, become more flexible and mobile. The co-ordination of representations indicates the appearance of mental operations.

The child moves from the preoperational to the operational stage.

Which are there more of, Freddy, plastic buttons or black buttons?

There are more black ones. Can't you see there are only two white ones?

Are the white ones plastic buttons?

Yes.

And the black ones?

Yes.

So, are there more black ones or plastic ones?

There are more black ones.

Only when Freddy can perform operations which allow him to group mentally the buttons into three classes (white buttons, black buttons and the inclusive class: plastic buttons) will he be able to do this reasoning correctly. In addition, he will be able to solve the reverse: plastic buttons minus white buttons equals black buttons. To do this, he will have to compare the parts (black buttons or white buttons) with the whole (plastic buttons). Now, he can only compare part with part. When one of them is removed, the whole ceases to exist for the child.

Mandy, 8 years old, has no difficulty with this experiment. She is able to understand that there is an inclusive class (plastic buttons) and that she can create new classes (black buttons and white buttons) whilst maintaining the inclusive class at the same time. She can compare the part with the whole.

148

So, as we've seen, an operation is...

> ...an internalized action (usually called thought). It has as its origin a group of physical actions which have become mental representations. These are co-ordinated and have certain interrelated properties, for example: irreversibility.

So how are effective actions and thought (internalized actions) different?

Thought originates with real, effective action, with contact with things and when it becomes abstract thought, it doesn't lose its essential quality, it is still action.

> Pick me up, Mum!

> I started wrong. I'll do it again.

- ○ Actions are those which are based on objects (playing the piano) or on the organism itself (moving around). In some cases, actions can take place in opposite directions, in others it is not always easy to return to the point of departure.
- ○ Thought is capable of making the irreversible reversible and of ordering thoughts in order to overcome the limits of effective action.

But what is thought?

- ○ A succession of images
- ○ Any representation
- ○ A chain of association

- ○ An act of solidarity with others
- ○ Together they constitute a system

The specific quality of thought is its reversibility

The concrete operations stage (6/7 to 10/11 years)

Mental operations give this period enormous possibilities. The child, capable of operating with the symbolic systems of language and mathematics, acquires a mechanism which liberates her from the world of perceived objects and from actions with objects. The symbols with which she operates leave the level of the private to become public.

However, the limitation has to do with the term 'concrete'. This indicates that the child still needs the presence of objects to reason. An example:

If Charles is less happy than Nicholas and happier than Thomas, who is the happiest of the three?

Lucy, who is in the concrete operations stage, cannot resolve a problem of this kind. She still isn't capable of carrying out the mental actions necessary to solve it. If she were allowed to touch objects or see the problem graphically, she would have no difficulty in working out steps which would lead to the answer.

Only later, from 11 or 12 years old, can she operate with abstract thought and replace real actions with virtual actions. These are what will permit her to assert the preservation of certain unchangeables, where perception shows modifications and variations.

In this period, which coincides with the beginning of children's primary schooling, dependency and obedience in relation to adult judgment, so much a part of early infancy, begin to change.

Emotions become more complex. Play and shared work give way to friendship and collaboration. Mutual respect progressively replaces obedience.

I was especially interested in the game of marbles because it is a children's game in which adults have no role. It also has very complex rules which are transmitted with a surprising inalterability from generation to generation.

Children at the preoperational period play marbles in any way they want. According to them, they are imitating adult rules, but really, they don't take any notice of them.

Children in the operational period submit to a number of precise and co-ordinated rules.

But how are these rules represented, and what do children feel about them?

> Imagine that one of you has invented a new rule which everyone accepts. Would it be a 'real rule'?

> No, the only rules are the ones that have always been there. Who invented them? It must have been the first man. No, better: God. Or maybe the President...

INCLUSIVE MORALITY

Any rule is respected as long as it is a product of an external will.

AUTONOMOUS MORALITY

At about 7 years of age, a rule is respected as long asit is the result of an explicit or tacit agreement.

> Yes, if we all agree, it can be a real rule.

The child child moves from concrete operations towards **formal opera-tions**. An operation represents different types of realities:

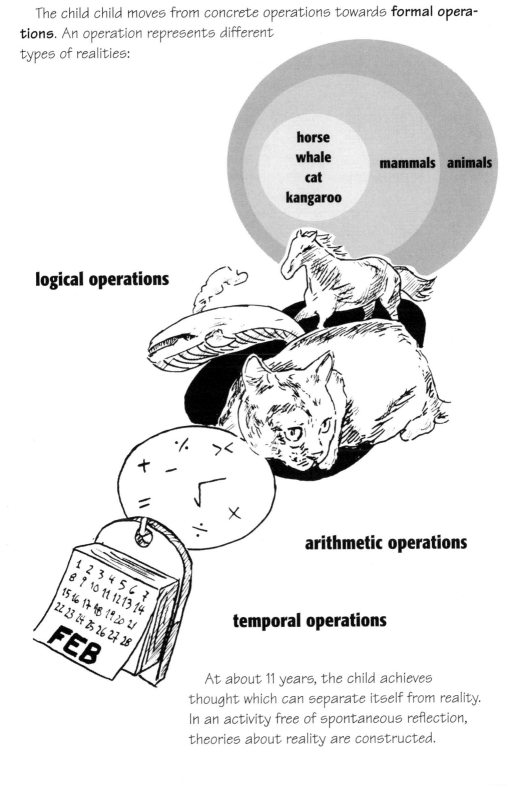

horse
whale
cat
kangaroo

mammals   animals

logical operations

arithmetic operations

temporal operations

At about 11 years, the child achieves thought which can separate itself from reality. In an activity free of spontaneous reflection, theories about reality are constructed.

The formal operations stage (11 years and beyond)

In this stage, children detach themselves from the immediate information and can reason not only about the real but also about the possible. They possess a logical framework which can be applied to any content. In addition, they can express thought through different languages: words, numbers, graphic symbols, etc.

As always, first comes egocentric assimilation. Adolescents discover the infinite power of reflection, and, in principle, reality must submit to their schemas of understanding.

As always, then comes adaptation. When a reconciliation between thought and reality is achieved, a new equilibrium is reached. Reflection is applied not only to contradict, but also to anticipate and interpret experience.

This new power of reflection implies a greater equilibrium than that of concrete thought. Why? Because it includes constructions of internal life and, at the same time, of the real.

Thanks to a double conquest, that of personality and the entry into adult society, affective and social life come closer during adolescence to what they will be in the future.

17 More than a century of Piaget

○ The work of Piaget consists of more than 50 books, numerous monographs and hundreds of articles. About 20,000 pages, translated into 18 languages, make Piaget (almost) as much quoted as Freud.

○ His theory is still the most complete in respect of mental development. It is also one of the most complex and interdisciplinary.

○ His work inspires work on the psychology of development.

○ Constructivism, the central thesis of Piagetian theory, was sketched out at the beginning of his work and developed in the 70s.

○ Teachers, especially those outside Switzerland, quote him frequently as one of the contemporary authors who has revolutionised ideas about education.

○ Like all great work, his is the object of numerous critics.

In psychology, theories which explain different phenomena are often seen as competing, thus losing the possibility of a fruitful dialogue. In many cases, Piaget was expected to account for aspects which his theory never intended to explain. And yet, because of this, there is an attempt to invalidate his contributions.

More than a hundred years after Piaget's birth, psychologists declare themselves to be Piagetians or anti-Piagetians, theories of knowledge or epistemologies are defined as constructivist-interactionist or the opposite.

Since this discipline was not central to his study, why, in the 60s and 70s, did it overshadow specialists in education?

Because his idea that a child, however small, possesses enormous creativity constituted an alternative to the conductivist vision of the time. This held that knowledge was transferred through language and that learning was a kind of storage or reproduction.

What did Piaget say to teachers?

Whoever wants to be a teacher must be a creator of opportunities for discovery. Teaching cannot be thought of as a mechanical, dogmatic practice. In this context, would it be a contradiction if practical teaching, derived from constructivism, were a 'recipe' which indicates at what age to teach things?

And couldn't Piaget's theory be applied in the classroom?

Yes, but they made the mistake of applying it directly.

What would be the risk of doing that?

For example, avoiding teaching a child something 'before time', because that is what is indicated as the age at which the operational structure appears, or taking experimental situations created by the Geneva School as teaching models.

What did Jean Piaget think about this?

He said that psychologists can't put themselves in the place of teachers to give then advice, but they can give them some ideas to consider.

But is it possible to take some kind of guidance from the theory?

Yes; for example, ensuring that in organising learning situations the pupil has a central role in his learning; defending teaching as a process which generates significant, not mechanical or repetitive learning; thinking of the mistake as a possibility and a condition for learning and not as a lack or ignorance based on the pupil's previous ideas.

Creativity: creating to understand; the world is comprehensible only insofar as the mind creates instruments to interpret it. He himself gave a lesson in creativity; having a different mentality to ordinary scientists, he offered a new model. He also gave a lesson in constructivism because he showed in his work that there are many worlds. The world can be reflected in a thousand ways in the eyes of each observer. The world is a place in which to be active.

Jean Piaget tried to disentangle the mechanisms through which human knowledge is formed and transformed. He hoped thus, without belonging to the philosophical community, to clarify the problem of knowledge, which is the central concern of modern philosophy.

He proposed a theoretical model of what happens within the subject, which cannot be observed directly, but can be seen through its consequences.

Genetic psychology is an inexhaustible source of ideas and principles which still inspire research and educational practice. At the same time, in the field of education, after a certain amount of exaggerated optimism regarding the possibilities of applying it directly, some of its limitations begin to be seen.

Constructivist theory, of great usefulness and great potential, is still being successfully applied in some fields such as teacher training (social sciences and reading/writing, for example), in research and in practical educational psychology...

Piaget was 'in fashion' during the 1970s and 1980s. There are those who predict a revival of his theories in the psychology of the 21st century. According to the most seasoned specialists, his work has not been overtaken by any comparable work with the same theoretical depth. It still constitutes a promising programme of research.

Nonetheless, and although it may appear paradoxical, the death of Piaget leaves a vacuum in epistemological research.

'To think, one must be many people.'

Curiously, although he said this, Piaget was a great loner. A man whose capacity for penetrating into the most diverse areas of knowledge engendered admiration in specialists who didn't always agree with him. Perhaps he is one of the last representatives of a lineage which includes men like Descartes and Leibnitz. That lineage is made up of those rare geniuses who contributed to the creation of science and revolutionised philosophy by having contributed to both fields.

Bibliography

Books by Jean Piaget

The Child's Conception of Movement and Speed

The Child's Conception of Number

The Child's Conception of Space, (tr. F.J. Langon & J.L. Lunzer), W.W. Norton, 1996

The Child's Conception of Time

The Child's Conception of the World, Littlefield Adams, 1990

The Child's Construction of Quantities: Conservation and Atomism

Construction of Reality in the Child

Children's Way of Knowing

The Development of Thought: Equilibration of Cognitive Structures

The Essential Piaget (Howard E. Gruber & J. Jacques Voneche eds), Praeger Pub, 1982

Genetic Epistemology

The Growth of Logical Thinking from Childhood to Adolescence

Judgment and Reasoning in the Child

The Language and Thought of the Child

The Mechanisms of Perception

Memory and Intelligence

Mental Imagery in the Child: A Study of the Development of Imagination

The Moral Judgment of the Child (tr. Marjorie Gabain), Free Press, 1985

The Origin of the idea of Chance in Children

Origins of Intelligence in Children, International Universities Press, 1992

Play, Dreams and Imitation in Childhood

Principles of Genetic Epistemology

The Psychology of Intelligence, Littlefield Adams, 1981

The Psychology of the Child (tr. Helen Weaver), Basic Books, 2000

Six Psychological Studies (tr. Anita Tenzer, ed. David Elkind), Random House, 1968

Books about Jean Piaget

Brainerd, C.J.: *Piaget's Theory of Intelligence*, Prentice Hall Inc, 1978

Bybee, Rodger W. & Sund, Robert B.: *Piaget for Educators*, Waveland Press, 1990

Campbell, S.F.: *A Piaget Sampler: An Introduction to Jean Piaget Through His Own Words*, Jason Aronson, 1987

Chapman, Michael: *Constructive Evolution: Origins and Development of Piaget's Thought*, Cambridge University Press, 1988

Droz, R-Emy: *Understanding Piaget*, International Universities Press, 1976

Elkind, David: *Child Development and Education: A Piagetian Perspective* Oxford University Press, 1976

Evans, Richard Isadore: *Dialogue with Jean Piaget*, Praeger Pub, 1982

Gruber, H.E. & Voneche J.J. (eds): *The Essential Piaget*, Basic Books, 1977

Isaacs, N.: *A Brief Introduction to Piaget*, Agathon Press, 1960

Jacob, S.H.: *Foundations for Piagetian Education*, University Press of America, 1985

Kitchener, Richard F.: *Piaget's Theory of Knowledge*, Yale University Press, 1986

Singer, Dorothy G. & Revenson, Tracey A.: *A Piaget Primer: How a Child Thinks*, New American Library, 1989

Vidal, Fernando: *Piaget Before Piaget*, Harvard University Press, 1994

Index

The Authors

Adriana Serulnikov is a qualified teacher with a degree in educational sciences. She is a consultant to educational institutes and designs teaching materials. The author of textbooks for adults and children, she has devoted a number of years to working in educational psychology and now extends her range to include physical therapy.

Rodrigo Suárez is a young Argentinian cartoonist who has studied with Alberto Salinas and Claudio Aboy. He has worked with the review AZ 10 as well as with a number of publishers of educational books.

Acknowledgements

This book is dedicated to: Pablo and our children Tomás, Lucía, Camilo and Nicolás for, once again, supporting my projects with kindness and love; to my brother Claudio who left us as these pages were taking shape. His creative spirit and his loving looks accompanied me through this work; to his son Julián who arrived soon after to begin his life and, without knowing it, to illuminate ours. Thanks especially to Estela Soriano who, with her unconditional help simplified this task; to the Swiss Embassy in Argentina for the loan of 'Jean Piaget Travelling Exhibition - A Celebration of the Centenary of His Birth'; to Emilio Ferreiro for his splendid work 'Los hombres' which awakened my youthful enthusiasm for Piaget; and to Chía Rodríguez for his confidence and assistance. - A.S.

This book is dedicated to María Bogetti: thank you, thank you, thank you for the explanations, your generous companionship, stimulation... and for everything; and to my parents. - R.S.

The editor wishes to thank Eduardo Newark for the assistance offered at the start of this book and for the illustration on page 1. - J.C.K.

accept no substitute!

> Great ideas and great thinkers can be thrilling. They can also be intimidating.

That's where **Writers and Readers** *For Beginners*™ books come in. **Writers and Readers** brought you the *very first For Beginners*™ book over twenty years ago. Since then, amidst a growing number of imitators, we've published some 80 titles (ranging from Architecture to Zen and Einstein to Elvis) in the internationally acclaimed *For Beginners*™ series. Every book in the series serves one purpose: to UNintimidate and UNcomplicate the works of the great thinkers. Knowledge is too important to be confined to the experts.

And knowledge, as you will discover in our **Documentary Comic Books,** is fun! Each book is painstakingly researched, humorously written and illustrated in whatever style best suits the subject at hand. That's where **Writers and Readers** *For Beginners*™ books began! Remember if it doesn't say...

Writers and Readers ®

...it's not an original *For Beginners* book.

To order any of the books or for a free catalog, please call:
(212) 941-0202 in the U.S or (020) 7226 2522 in the U.K.

what's

ARTAUD FOR BEGINNERS™
Gabriela Stoppelman
Illustrated by
Jorge Hardmeier
ISBN 0-86316-291-6

US $11.95
UK £7.99

Artaud for Beginners™ reveals the life and art of the man known in the avant-garde world as a "totally rebellious artist." His book, *The Theater and Its Double*, was first published in 1938, and is still considered one of the most important contributions to 20th century theater. Leading figures in the theater have attempted to turn into practice some aspects of Artaud's theory on drama, such as his "cruelty theory."

Artaud's "cruelty" aspires to a type of theater where the language of physical movement and gesture could be applied on a multitude of psychological levels. Artaud's intention was to abolish the boundaries between life and art. He applies this criterion to all his artistic productions, including: poetry, cinema, drawing and painting.

It is impossible to classify his books by specific genres, because he broke all genre rules. From his poems, *The Umbilicus of Limbo* and *The Nerve Meter*, to his most mature works such as *Van Gogh: The Man Suicided by Society*, Artaud rejected the acceptable and palatable conventions of traditional theater that serve to limit or mask the real torment of human suffering.

Artaud had suffered from illness since he was a small boy; later in life he endured drug addiction, rehabilitation treatments, nine years confinement in a series of psychiatric hospitals, and electroshock therapy. None of the horror that Artaud experienced in his life prevented him from gaining international recognition for his contribution to the art and theater worlds.

BUKOWSKI FOR BEGINNERS™
Carlos Polimeni
Illustrated by Miguel Rep
ISBN 0-86316-285-1

US $11.95
UK £7.99

Bukowski for Beginners™ examines the life and literary achievements of this unique American writer. Charles Bukowski is a cult figure of the dissident and rebellious, novelist, short story writer, poet and journalist.

Bukowski was born in Germany in 1920 and died in the United States in 1994. He was one of the most unconventional writers and cultural critics of the 20th century. Bukowski lived his life in his own way and wrote in a style that was impossible to classify or categorize. His work is cynical at times and humorous at others, but always brilliant, and always challenging. His life and work is distinguished not only by this remarkable talent for words, but also his rejection of the dominate social and cultural values of American Society—the American Dream.

Bukowski began writing at the age of 40, and during that time he published 45 books, six of them novels. Along with Raymond Chandler and Joan Didion, he is a great voice of Los Angeles and Southern California; an area full of contradictions and chimeras hidden beneath the masquerade of wealth and progress.

new?

DANTE FOR BEGINNERS™
Joe Lee
ISBN 0-86316-280-0

US $11.95
UK £7.99

At long last, a Divine Comedy with jokes, a Dante with shtick, a trip through the afterlife with a happy ending. Actually it always had a happy ending, but who could have known that after *The Inferno* comes *Purgatorio* and *Paradiso*? **Dante for Beginners™** takes the reader on a trip starting in hell and ending in heaven. The reader gets a quick introduction to Dante and his times (you always wanted to know a Guelph from a Ghibelline, didn't you?). Next, the reader meets a sweet lass named Beatrice (whose face may not have launched a thousand ships, but certainly caused Dante to dip his oar in the ink), and sample a bit of his other literary offerings, such as the great feast, *The Convivio*. But then it is on to the big one, *The Commedia*, and a canto by canto description of the entire work. Characters, ideas and situations are described as they happen–no searching through end notes, footnotes or field notes to distinguish Forese Donati, Dante's pal, from his evil brother, Corso. The entire plan of the hereafter is simply mapped out. **Dante for Beginners™** is a great vacation with history's greatest tourist, Dante Alighieri. Pack a bag for the thrills and ills of Hell, Purgatory's sweet salvation and the hallucinogenic high of heaven.

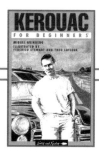

KEROUAC FOR BEGINNERS™
Miguel Grinberg
Illustrated by
Frederico Stuart and
Theo Lafleur
ISBN 0-86316-287-8

US $11.95
UK £7.99

Jack Kerouac (1922-1969) is not only one of the major writers of the United States after World War II, but also the best known figure of the Beat Generation. "The Beats" were portrayed by Kerouac in his best selling novel *On the Road* as aesthetic pilgrims—pilgrims who were "mad to live, mad to talk, mad to be saved." Kerouac and his contemporaries used this madness to test the boundaries of everything: frenetic sex, writing, living, Zen Buddhism, fast cars, freight trains and be-bop Jazz.

Kerouac for Beginners™ is a journey into the world of Kerouac's major novels and poems. Kerouac is accompanied on his short, but fast paced journey by other visionaries like Allen Ginsburg and William S. Burroughs. Through their literary and lifestyle experimentation, Kerouac and his fellow Beats laid down the foundation for the more wide spread cultural revolution of the hippies in the 1960s.

How to get original thinkers to come to your home...

Individual Orders

US
Writers and Readers Publishing, Inc.
P.O. Box 461, Village Station
New York, NY 10013
Phone: 212.941.0202
Fax: 212.941.0011
sales@forbeginners.com
www.writersandreaders.com

UK
Writers and Readers Ltd.
PO Box 29522
London N1 8FB
Phone: 020 7226 2522
Fax: 020 7359 1406
begin@writersandreaders.com
www.writersandreaders.com

Trade Orders

US
Publishers Group West
1700 Fourth St.
Berkeley, CA 94710
Phone: 800.788.3123
Fax: 510.528.9555

Canada
Publishers Group West
250 A Carlton St.
Toronto, Ontario M5A2LI
Phone: 800.747.8147

UK
Littlehampton Book Services Ltd.
Faraday Close
Durrington
Worthing, West Sussex BN13 3RB
Phone: 01903 828800
Fax: 01903 828802
orders@lbsltd.co.uk

South Africa
Real Books
5 Mortlake St.
Brixton, 2092
Phone: 2711 837 0643
Fax: 2711 837 0645

Australia
Tower Books
Unit 9/19 Rodborough Rd.
French Forest NSW 2086
Phone: 02 9975 5566
Fax: 02 9975 5599

SHIP TO (NAME)

ADDRESS

CITY   STATE   ZIP

COUNTRY

TELEPHONE (DAY)   (EVENING)

To request a free catalog, check here: ☐

Title	Quantity	Amount
SUBTOTAL		
New York City residents add 8.25% sales tax		
Shipping & Handling: Add $3.50 for 1st book, $.60 for each additional book		
TOTAL PAYMENT		